KENSINGTON PALACE

AN INTIMATE MEMOIR FROM
Queen Mary to Meghan Markle

TOM QUINN

\Bᵇ\
Biteback Publishing

This paperback edition published in Great Britain in 2020 by
Biteback Publishing Ltd, London
Copyright © Tom Quinn 2020, 2021

Tom Quinn has asserted his right under the Copyright, Designs and Patents Act 1988
to be identified as the author of this work.

ISBN 978-1-78590-647-3

10 9 8 7 6 5 4 3 2 1

A CIP catalogue record for this book is available from the British Library.

Set in Bulmer

Printed and bound in Great Britain by
CPI Group (UK) Ltd, Croydon CR0 4YY

MIX
Paper from
responsible sources
FSC
www.fsc.org   FSC® C020471

CONTENTS

PREFACE

*'It has been said ... with a possible approximation to truth, that in
1802 every hereditary monarch in Europe was insane.'*
WALTER BAGEHOT, *THE ENGLISH CONSTITUTION*, 1867

'What is she for?'
WILLY HAMILTON MP ON PRINCESS MARGARET

Kensington Palace was the centre of court life in England from
1690 to 1760. During those years, anyone who wanted to influence the monarch or obtain favours from him (or her) for themselves
or for relatives and friends had to live near or at Kensington Palace.
Ministers and aristocrats, friends and relatives, those in search of work
or preferment, had no choice but to travel down the Kensington road
to what was then a small village west of London.

After 1760 the court left Kensington never to return, and Kensington
Palace became home to the relatives and friends of succeeding monarchs. Some of its residents were part of the immediate royal family;

others were more distantly related. Many residents were simply aristocrats who were deemed to have served the royal family in some capacity.

Rows and scheming, family disputes, petty squabbles over precedence, ancient feuds and bitterness – for the royals and others, these have always been part of life at Kensington Palace.

When the court was at Kensington, the palace was the centre of political power as it was where ministers met and consulted with the monarch, but it was also the centre of the royal family's lives; today, though the court is no longer at Kensington and royal power has ebbed away, the palace remains very much central to the lives of the coming generation of royals, especially William, the future king.

This book provides a unique, intimate look at the lives of today's young royals, and also charts the lives of those who have lived at the palace throughout its history; but this is not a record of what, officially, went on. It is a history, if you like, of personal relationships. Bland official accounts often skim the surface of troubled lives and difficult relationships; they tone down tales of the mad, the bad and the dangerous to know. This book does the opposite by looking behind the scenes at the lives and loves of Kensington Palace residents and their servants down the ages, all viewed within the context of an ancient building that has only ever been partly open to the public.

In the seventeenth century, for example, when King William III and his wife Mary lived at Kensington, they got on very badly with Mary's sister Anne, who hated the fact that William and Mary viewed Anne's husband, Prince George of Denmark, as a complete nonentity. They lived together at Kensington Palace and were formally and superficially polite to each other, but it is easy to imagine the tears and tantrums behind the facade. More recently, in an echo of that long-vanished relationship, the sisters-in-law – Catherine, Duchess of Cambridge and Meghan, Duchess of Sussex – found themselves caught up in a similarly complex dynamic of kindness mixed with bitterness and jealousies. At Kensington there is nothing new under the sun.

Down the long years between 1760, when the monarch moved away from Kensington to Buckingham Palace, and the present era, the story of Kensington is the story of the minor royals, the more distant relatives and their countless servants who lived and died at the palace; rowing with each other, squabbling over precedence and position, but all the while keeping a beautiful and interesting building alive.

INTRODUCTION

'She will have to walk behind the angels – and she won't like that.'
EDWARD VII ON BEING ASKED IF HIS MOTHER WOULD BE HAPPY IN HEAVEN

'You can't treat royalty like people with normal perverted desires.'
TOM STOPPARD, *ROSENCRANTZ AND GUILDENSTERN ARE DEAD*

At various times in its history, Kensington Palace has come under real threat of demolition. The most serious threat, during the second half of the nineteenth century, was averted only when Queen Victoria insisted that her birthplace should not be destroyed. But her motivation was not entirely based on sentiment. She was shrewd enough to realise that without Kensington Palace there would be nowhere suitable in London to house all those near and distant relatives she wished either to patronise or to control (or both). It was this role – as the 'house of the hangers-on', as one journalist put it – that Edward VII famously echoed when he described Kensington Palace as 'the aunt heap'.

In a sense this book is an account of the aunt heap. Here you will discover the stories of those aunts and many others who have been forgotten for too long in the effort to focus always on the immediate royal family; as the journalist Peter Mahone put it, here you will find the 'dotty and the potty', in a story that takes us from the early seventeenth century right up to the tempestuous years when Princess Margaret lived at the palace, and beyond, to the present day.

I have included some anecdotes that are not directly related to Kensington simply because they are funny or extraordinary or provide a neat insight into the lives of the early Hanoverians who loved the palace. Some of these stories are bizarre, at least by today's standards – we forget, for example, that royal couples were public property in earlier centuries in a way that would be unthinkable now. So it was not strange at all when George II and Princess Caroline of Ansbach, on their wedding night, dressed only in their nightshirts, found themselves surrounded by courtiers, lords, ladies, servants and even strangers who watched the couple climb nervously into bed and then made extremely bawdy remarks until ushered out of the room. Or take the fact that Queen Victoria sent a telegram each month to her doctor informing him that 'the bowels are acting fully'.

For a writer, the Hanoverians and their favourite palace are almost too good to be true – and this is especially so when one considers the outliers, those most likely to find themselves tucked away at Kensington. George III's daughter Elizabeth, for example, was married aged forty-eight to a massively obese German widower called Frederick, Landgrave of Hesse-Homburg (known to all and sundry as Humbug). According to Karl Shaw in *Oddballs and Eccentrics*, Frederick was forced to wash immediately before his nuptials as he stank, and as he and his bride drove away in their coach after the wedding, he threw up all over her.

Much of my information about the past fifty years of Kensington Palace's history comes from a series of interviews I conducted with servants at the palace. In the 1970s, servants were willing – sometimes positively eager – to talk about their lives, and this situation lasted well into the 1990s. It has been more difficult to source information in recent times, as those who work for the royal family now have to sign confidentiality agreements, but people still like to talk off the record about their lives, especially their working lives, whatever the barriers and risks. This book is the result of that desire to talk.

Kensington Palace's history is as much to do with the characters who lived and worked at the palace as it is to do with bricks and mortar, and this is especially true of the palace's most famous resident, the late Diana, Princess of Wales. Her disastrous marriage to Prince Charles was played out in all its horror at Kensington. The bitterness of that relationship has echoes of other ancient and not-so-ancient royal couplings.

These unhappy marriages, based largely on the absurd idea that royals should marry only other royals (or at least aristocrats), have had at least one positive outcome. The royal family has explicitly acknowledged that the world has changed, and that welcoming commoners and divorcees into the family in a way that would have been unimaginable even half a century ago has created a more open institution, which has helped to deflect republican criticism. Of course, allowing outsiders to marry in also suggests a royal family that is prepared to live dangerously. The divorced, mixed-race Meghan Markle is testament to a remarkably changed world. But then American divorcees, as history teaches us, can lead to royal disasters.

This book developed out of a conversation with a friend who had worked for a short time in the kitchens at Kensington Palace. He was an ardent socialist and had taken the job only out of desperation. Inevitably he was outraged at the starvation wages he was paid and at the luxury in which those he served lived. His tiny wage packet was taxed and, in his eyes, it meant he was paying for a bunch of 'layabouts and dozy hangers-on' to live the sort of life about which he could only dream.

My friend neatly points out the difficulty with writing about the royal family and the places where they choose to live. Books on any and every aspect of the royals' lives tend to be split starkly into two categories: those that are embarrassingly deferential and those that attack and ridicule. As my friend would put it, 'Why in God's name is a dustman in Middlesbrough paying his taxes so that a large extended family of German extraction can be looked after by footmen, dressers, pages (including pages of the backstairs), ladies of the bedchamber and numerous other domestic servants and skivvies?'

It's an impossible question to answer other than to say that the dustman may very well be more than happy to pay for this dream world.

The royal family is like a complex mechanical toy, kitted out with fictional characters living in a world that has largely vanished. They have to live like this, or we will lose a much-loved fantasy; a fantasy that has replaced the supernatural belief once reserved for the church. As the great political writer Walter Bagehot put it, 'Above all things our royalty is to be reverenced, and if you begin to poke about it, you cannot reverence it … Its mystery is its life. We must not let daylight in upon magic.'

This book tries to steer a middle course between deference and disapproval. No one can doubt that the royal family brings vast amounts of money to the UK via tourism, perhaps even more money than it costs the taxpayer to keep the family in the style to which they have long been accustomed. Through traditional ceremony and pageantry, the existence of the royal family also adds immensely to the gaiety of the nation and, astonishing though it may seem to some, there has never been a serious attempt to remove the British royal family in the way that so many other European royal families have been removed.

Despite the foolish belief among many royal apologists that the modern press is critical of the royal family in a manner quite unprecedented, the truth is very different. Modern attacks on the royals are actually rather mild compared to the savagery of the early eighteenth century, when a caricature was published showing the Prince Regent defecating over France.

It was only in the middle decades of the twentieth century that it became very bad form to criticise the royals – when, for example, John Grigg (later to abjure his right to sit in the House of Lords as Lord Altrincham) criticised the recently crowned Elizabeth II for surrounding herself with tweedy old Etonians, a man rushed up in full view of the TV cameras and punched Grigg in the face. No one protested in a similar way when crowds booed Queen Victoria for refusing to open Parliament on the grounds that she was still in mourning thirty years after Albert's death; no one protested – or at least not much – when the mild-mannered Queen Charlotte, wife of George III, was regularly described as an 'old hag' (which she most definitely was not).

Most of the reforms suggested by John Grigg were gradually instituted – ironically, the one thing that hasn't changed is the royal family's insistence that all senior advisers and equerries should be tweedy aristocrats.

Make of it what you will, but to this day, not a single comprehensive school-educated man or woman has entered royal service as Master of the Household, Master of the Horse or in any other role as an equerry.

This book isn't meant to be an entirely serious study of Kensington Palace and those who lived and worked there. Serious studies are legion. The minutiae of the process by which the palace came into being and was altered over the centuries are not the focus of this book. There will be some of this, but only if it is in some way out of the ordinary. I want instead to cover the odd and the eccentric, the hidden and the strange, as well as the work of Christopher Wren, William Kent and the other architects and artists who had a hand in creating the Kensington Palace we see now.

To some, this book will seem unashamedly gossipy and therefore frivolous. It doesn't cover the slow process by which Lord Bute, for example, groomed the young George III; it doesn't cover in any detail the endless political discussions of George II's ministers at Kensington Palace; all this has been written about again and again. Instead, I have looked at what the servants – especially in more recent times – saw and how they functioned in the palace; I have looked at the whole idea of grace-and-favour apartments – essentially flats and houses that the monarch has always been entitled to give to near and distant relatives, favoured aristocratic servants and assorted hangers-on; I have looked most especially at the eccentric lives of lesser royals who lived, unknown and uncelebrated sometimes for decades, at Kensington Palace. I've looked through the eyes of the servants at the daily lives and machinations, pomposities and tendernesses of Charles and Diana, Princess Margaret and Antony Armstrong-Jones, Kate and William, Meghan and Harry.

I have always been drawn to eccentrics and nonconformists, and over the years Kensington Palace has housed them all; the lesser-known royals often turn out to be far nicer than more prominent members of the royal household. Princess Margaret and Lord Snowdon were famously awful – they shouted abuse at each other throughout much of their time at Kensington. Their endless, hateful rows were played out for all to hear. In earlier epochs quieter souls prevailed: George III's sixth son, the Duke of Sussex, spent decades hidden away at Kensington Palace with his vast collection of songbirds and dusty books and manuscripts – he was said to possess more than 5,000 volumes, including more than 1,000 early Bibles. Certainly, in the popular imagination, Kensington Palace was seen as a place to which the royal family sometimes sent its oddballs.

By the mid-nineteenth century, Kensington House, an old mansion on the opposite side of Kensington High Street from the palace itself, had been converted into a lunatic asylum and the joke among Londoners was that there was no way to tell whether the asylum was on the left or the right as you passed along the road.

✤

When Edward VII described Kensington Palace as the aunt heap, he was nothing if not accurate, for here the forgotten and sometimes notorious royals have lived, loved and died over the centuries, secure in the knowledge that as cousins and aunts they deserved the grace and favour bestowed on them. But what were their lives like as the palace crumbled around them or was repaired, remodelled and reshaped? If you'd like to know, then this is the book for you.

In earlier times the opinions of 'the lower sort' were considered unimportant, but as the great lexicographer Samuel Johnson explained to a friend writing a biography, the best way to find out someone's real character is to spend an hour talking to his servants.

There will be complaints, no doubt, that the book does not itemise sources for every quotation and comment. Readers who enjoy such things will be able to find them in more formal histories. I have listed my sources at the back of the book but without detailed and (I think) often distracting notes. The bulk of the material in the latter part of

the book does not have acknowledged sources because my inform-
ants were adamant they would not speak to me about their time at the
palace if any clue was given as to their identity. I have honoured my
promise to them in order to ensure that their memories do not vanish
into what Lytton Strachey called 'the long oblivion of history'.

Certainly, until fairly recently the views of 'ordinary' people – and
perhaps especially servants – would have been of no interest, but the
world has changed and we now recognise that deep insights do not
just come from the wealthy and powerful. For much of the period covered by this book, things were very different, of course. Just how different can be readily glimpsed through a story told by the philosopher
Bertrand Russell.

Russell recalled attending a meeting of pacifists in London in 1915.
The meeting was stormed by a club-wielding gang of pacifist haters
accompanied by the police. Many of those attending the meeting were
assaulted and badly hurt and Russell was about to be similarly attacked
when someone said to the police, who were standing by idly while the
attack took place, 'You really ought to do something. He [pointing at
Russell] is a distinguished writer.' The police did nothing. 'He is also
a distinguished philosopher.' Still the police did nothing.

'He is the brother of an earl.' The police immediately intervened to
save him from the mob.

The sense throughout most of the period covered by this book
that working people were inherently inferior existed alongside the
knowledge that the aristocracy could not survive without them. As the
Quaker John Bellers (1654–1725) put it, 'Regularly labouring people
are the kingdom's greatest treasure and strength, for without labourers

there can be no lords; and if the poor labourers did not raise much more food and manufacture than what did subsist themselves, every gentleman must be a labourer and every idle man must starve.'

In many ways, the idle rich – typically aristocratic landowners – were of less use even than the royal family, as the great nineteenth-century expert on the constitution Walter Bagehot suggested when he put forward the idea that the monarchy represents the 'dignified' element of government while the ministers and ruling party represent the 'efficient'.

The problem in recent times is that, with the notable and highly laudable exception of HM Queen Elizabeth II, the modern monarchy has failed to be dignified. Three out of four of the Queen's children are divorced and all of her children have become embroiled in embarrassing scandals: Prince Andrew had to explain away the fact that his former wife tried to sell access to him; far more seriously, in more recent times, he has had to give up all his royal duties following his failure to explain his long and apparently close relationship with the convicted paedophile Jeffrey Epstein, not to mention his alleged relationship with a number of young girls. One royal insider has said that Andrew is under pressure from the royal family to live abroad. The perception in royal circles is that he will never be able to rebuild public trust. Far less seriously, but still embarrassingly, Prince Charles has a history of trying to influence public policy (not to mention admitting to an adulterous relationship), while Edward used his royal status to further his career as a TV executive.

Of course, the Queen's admirable policy of 'never complain, never explain' is by no means typical of the royals. With the exception, perhaps, of George III and Queen Victoria, all the Hanoverian monarchs behaved in supremely undignified ways – fathering numerous illegitimate children, demanding huge amounts of money from Parliament for vanity projects and failing to pay their debts.

But, as we will see, it was ever thus.

CHAPTER ONE

BRICKS AND MORTAR

'I declare this thing open – whatever it is.'
PRINCE PHILIP, DUKE OF EDINBURGH

Those who write about architecture tend to be rather grand, with a few notable exceptions including the great Nikolaus Pevsner (1902–83), whose name has become synonymous with a certain kind of no-nonsense architectural writing. But then, Pevsner had been trained in the more vigorous, unsentimental German tradition. British architectural writers tend to talk rather pompously about the relationship between planes and volumes, as opposed to the more basic elements of building. No one, so far as I have been able to discover, has noted the simple fact about Kensington Palace that its bricks are laid in what is known as Flemish bond. This style would be obvious then and now to any bricklayer worth his salt.

Flemish bond was just coming into fashion when Kensington Palace was being remodelled by Christopher Wren towards the end of the seventeenth century. The technique for laying Flemish bond is as follows: a stretcher (a brick laid lengthways) is always followed by a header (a brick laid end on), then another stretcher and so on.

Traditionally, English brick buildings had been built using English bond where a line of bricks is laid end to end (stretchers) until the first line is completed. The next line (or 'course') of bricks are then all laid end on (headers) – i.e. at right angles to the first course. English bond is still considered stronger than Flemish bond and it is perhaps the use of the latter that has resulted, in part at least, in the endless repetition of the idea that Kensington Palace was jerry-built – in other words, built badly and too quickly using inferior materials. In fact, Kensington Palace was simply adopting the latest fashion in bricklaying. And much of the brickwork was putty jointed, which was very expensive. There were shortcuts, certainly – timber used and painted to resemble stone here and there, for example – but it was a mix of 'no expense spared' in some areas and 'cheap and cheerful' in others. The basic structure would have been little different from many other buildings of the time.

Architectural writers often talk about buildings being jerry-built when they don't like them or wish to justify their demolition. John Nash's magnificent Regent Street was destroyed in the 1920s on the grounds that so-called experts called it jerry-built – those same experts would no doubt recommend the complete rebuilding of Venice on the grounds that so many of its buildings are 'jerry-built' and sinking into the mud.

The 'jerry-built' criticism has been levelled at Kensington Palace over the years, and it almost led to the building's complete destruction in the nineteenth century.

Most of the stories of Kensington's structural inadequacies stem from the speed with which the palace was enlarged for William and Mary and the fact that on one occasion in November 1689 part of a wall collapsed. This may well have stemmed from overly hasty building, but there were no safety standards at the time and new techniques could be used only on a trial-and-error basis.

At Hampton Court, where more money and more time was available for work taking place around the same time, another wall collapsed, killing two workmen. In fact, this happened just a month after the Kensington Palace accident. The truth is that all early buildings are poorly built in some respects – they usually lack what we now consider 'proper' foundations, for example – but well-built in others. Rather than cheap softwood timbers, early buildings usually have oak and other hardwoods, for instance.

As part of the research for this book I spoke to an elderly man who had worked as a labourer when, in order to modernise the apartment destined to be lived in by Princess Margaret and Antony Armstrong-Jones, Christopher Wren's Stone Court at Kensington Palace was destroyed. Asked about the quality of the building work, John Fagan said:

> It was incredibly solidly built; absolutely solid brickwork throughout and beautifully put together. The thing about a really good bricklayer is that his work improves the faster he goes because he lays light and accurate when he gets into a really good swing of work. Those early bricklayers really knew what they were doing.

In truth, then, Kensington Palace was built just as solidly as many grand houses of the time. The 'poor quality' argument has always been a simple and not entirely honest device to justify removing early historic work in order to create modern apartments. If the palace became dilapidated at various times in its history, it was because it was abandoned, often for decades. Any building left that long without maintenance will begin to fall apart. In fact, it is testimony to the skills of the original workmen – carpenters and bricklayers, tilers and roofers – that the building is still there today despite the various long periods of neglect.

The real problem with Kensington Palace, if there is one, is that the original house was built on boggy ground – a spring reached a conduit house in the grounds until the nineteenth century and a number of streams flowed across the area where the house was built. A bigger stream a little to the east (the Westbourne) was later widened and deepened to form the Serpentine lake we see today.

The water didn't just create an unstable basis for Kensington (as it would for any house, however well-built); it also led to complaints that Kensington Palace, or parts of it, was unhealthy. The eighteenth-century diarist John Hervey recalled George II asking Queen Caroline to go to London from Kensington, 'that house where she was having the reputation of being damp…'

Certainly, the basement rooms were very damp in the early days – George II's mistress Henrietta Howard wrote to a friend that she could have grown mushrooms in her basement apartment at Kensington; but Henrietta would have known that putting her in those damp rooms was probably George's way of making it clear that she was a mistress, not a wife. She was important, but she should not get ideas above her station.

Damp certainly damages brickwork, especially early bricks, which were softer than their modern equivalent, so by the late nineteenth

4

century many of the walls at Kensington were leaning and had to be shored up thanks to the lowest courses of brick crumbling.

Very little of the original core of Kensington Palace remains today, not because it fell down as a result of shoddy workmanship or damp, but because the house bought by William and Mary – then known as Nottingham House – was remodelled and enlarged by Christopher Wren at the end of the seventeenth century in a rather odd way. Wren didn't rebuild from scratch because the royals were in a hurry and wanted to show that they were prepared to be careful with money taken from the public purse. William, the new king fresh from the Glorious Revolution, wished to demonstrate that he was both frugal and prudent with the resources of his new kingdom.

The story of the original house has often been told, but a brief account may be in order. Around 1610, Sir Walter Cope was offered the lucrative job of Keeper of Hyde Park. It was largely a sinecure and Cope did not expect to have to do any work himself. He kept his large annual salary and paid small sums to others to guard the gates and maintain the fences. By the time he had been made keeper, Cope already owned the land where Kensington Palace now stands. But when he died in 1614, he owed so much money that his widow was forced to sell some of his estate. The land where the palace is now was sold to Sir George Coppin. By 1618 Coppin had built a simple though probably rather beautiful house, of which a single drawing survives. Historians describe it as small, but by today's standards it was by no means small. It was a roughly square house with a central entrance leading to a large hall that ran from front to back. At either side of the great hall were other reception rooms – a parlour, for example. In the basement were servants' rooms, a kitchen and various storerooms.

The first floor was divided into a series of bedrooms and there were more servants' bedrooms in the attic. The house had bay windows and stepped or Dutch gables. The architect was almost certainly John Thorpe, who was famous for designing houses with corridors rather than adhering to the older system of building rooms that opened into each other. Thorpe also designed Lord Cecil's huge house at Audley End in Essex and Cope Castle, later known as Holland House, built just a mile or so west of Kensington House. Holland House was severely damaged by German bombs during the Second World War and only one wing now survives.

Sir George Coppin died in 1620 and the house passed to his widow, who sold it to Sir Heneage Finch in 1628.

Finch, a lawyer and later speaker of the English House of Commons, whose son was to become Lord Chancellor and Earl of Nottingham, enjoyed his new purchase for just three years before he died in 1631. His widow, Elizabeth, lived on in the house, which was considered to have been designed in the latest fashion at the time, for thirty years. When she died in 1661 the house was bought by Sir Heneage's eldest son, who, confusingly, was also called Heneage.

Samuel Pepys visited the house in 1664. In 1682, when the second Sir Heneage Finch died, the house – by now known as Nottingham House – was inherited by another Finch, Daniel, second Earl of Nottingham, who then sold it to King William III in 1689. Finch decided that his family and staff – more than sixty in all – needed more space than Nottingham House could provide. He was no doubt delighted to find a ready buyer in King William, who paid 18,000 guineas (around £20,000) for the house and grounds. But why was William so keen to buy a house just two miles from his far grander palace at Whitehall?

Apparently William, who suffered from asthma, hated the rambling, damp, smoky palace of Whitehall. Nottingham House would have seemed a rural idyll – surrounded by fields and meadows, unpolluted by tens of thousands of coal fires and a river reeking of sewage. The village of Kensington was at that time little more than a hamlet.

A newly built house away from the river but still in London might have offered a different solution, but apart from the fact that William did not want to be seen as profligate, there simply wasn't room. According to the architect John James, writing in 1712:

> A late years the town is so increased and tenement buildings so much run on that most of the great houses that belonged to people of quality are thrown down and turned into tenements and there is hardly to be got ground about the town fit for people of quality to build houses in.

Kensington appealed to William and Mary because it was close enough to London without being hemmed in (or bordered by a dirty river) and it reminded them of Het Loo, their palace in the Netherlands. But if Nottingham House was delightfully situated, it was also far too small for a king.

So William employed Christopher Wren, then at the height of his fame, to make the house bigger. This was quicker and cheaper than pulling the old house down and rebuilding. Wren came up with an ingenious solution. He built four small square houses (or pavilions) at each corner of the original house. Like most architects, he would probably have preferred to start from scratch and demolish the old house, but William would have none of it and insisted that the house must simply be enlarged. Adding four corner houses was a neat solution that

7

satisfied the king's desire for a speedy enlargement. It also meant that at a later stage the central part of the palace – the original old house – could be rebuilt while the corner pavilions continued to accommodate the royal household.

Over the years, as with most old houses, the palace was to be hacked about and remodelled; staircases were moved and whole areas of Wren's work ripped out as late as the 1960s. But for William and Mary and, following their deaths, Queen Anne, Kensington Palace became an adored home and, despite changes to other parts of the palace, the great state rooms where they lived have survived, largely unaltered, to this day.

But what of the early inhabitants of the house transformed into a palace?

William and Mary seem positively sane in comparison with the royals who were to succeed them; for instance, Anne, whose loss of seventeen children – all stillborn or failing to survive childhood – made her decidedly odd and unhappy. Scandalously, she was rumoured to have enjoyed a close (possibly sexual) relationship with the Duchess of Marlborough. But the real madness sets in with the Hanoverians who followed Anne; they set a standard for eccentric and scandalous behaviour unmatched until recent times.

Kensington Palace was the scene of much of this eccentricity and the house itself was considered an outlandish choice for a monarch. Many thought it entirely unsuitable for a king even in its rebuilt form, but as Peter Thorold points out in his book *The London Rich*, 'Kensington Palace can be seen in a sense as a replacement for the vanished Richmond and Nonsuch [Palaces] and the others ... and it was more convenient especially in winter than Windsor and Hampton Court.'

Kensington's great virtue was not its size, or its grand imposing rooms, or its magnificent grounds. It was simply a question of location.

Certainly, after the abolition of the monarchy in 1649 several palaces were entirely or partly destroyed, including Sheen and Nonsuch. Kensington was closer to London than those palaces that remained, as Thorold rightly explains, and it may be that, being smaller, Kensington also fitted rather better with the new idea of a monarch who could no longer spend almost unlimited amounts of money, just as he could no longer exercise almost unlimited power.

Complaints that Kensington (even with its pavilions) was not really magnificent enough for the dignity of the monarch reached a pitch in 1712 with a plan to build a much bigger palace in nearby Hyde Park – perhaps one rather like Versailles – but nothing came of it, probably because William was happy enough at Kensington House. This would have enhanced the image of him as a reasonable, modern monarch. Mary insisted in a letter to a friend that the king had originally bought Nottingham House as a way to appease the courtiers who wanted him to remain at Whitehall so that they would not have to travel far to see him – Hampton and Windsor were, they insisted, too far away. But once he was at Kensington there were still complaints. Sir Charles Sedley told the House of Commons that the courtiers kept William at Kensington Palace 'as in a box'.

From surviving accounts, Queen Mary appears to have been central to Christopher Wren's work at Kensington, perhaps because William was away much of the time fighting in Ireland and in France. William, it seems, only really felt at home when he was away from home. But Mary seems to have genuinely loved Kensington and she was concerned that Wren's rebuilding should be well done. She lived at nearby Holland

House while the work at Kensington continued and visited regularly to check progress.

William and Mary no doubt enjoyed what they would have seen as their rural retreat, but they also would have known that, for them, a genuine retreat was impossible. Several hundred courtiers, including the Lord Chamberlain, Master of the Horse, Groom of the Stool, Lord Privy Seal and countless others expected to be housed at the palace, along with their numerous servants.

Although the palace has been derided by some architectural historians as an unfortunate muddle, the lack of symmetry in its overall appearance is pleasing to the casual observer as Kensington has an almost organic quality – a sense, like many older English houses, of having been added to and altered over the years to create something unique and original rather than something strictly planned and coherent from the outset.

A passer-by will not mind that the East Front and South Front of the house are rather different from each other, nor that Wren added a long wing stretching westwards to house offices and kitchens. Stables were also added and remain to this day (although they were largely rebuilt in the twentieth century).

Interestingly, Wren asked another great architect of the period, Nicholas Hawksmoor – perhaps best known as the architect of London's Christ Church, Spitalfields – to supervise the day-to-day progress of the work, and as a result we even know the names of many of the workmen, carpenters, stonemasons and bricklayers: Thomas Hughes and later Richard Stacey were in charge of masonry and brickwork; the chief plasterer was Henry Margetts; the carpenter, Matthew Banks. More famously, the woodcarver Grinling Gibbons (1648–1721) contributed to the palace and some of his extraordinary work survives there to this day. Despite the involvement of two of the greatest architects of the time, much of the decorative work was done quickly – doorcases and external carvings were cleverly made from timber painted to look like stone. But these attempts at cutting corners were largely concerned with decorative elements.

No one could complain that the grand solid oak staircase was shoddily built – yet it was damaged when, following her death from smallpox in 1694, Mary's lead coffin was carried downstairs.

Mary's linked state rooms were complete in the form we see them today by 1692. The king's rooms – including the splendid long gallery, which also survives – were completed much later, after Mary's death.

Complaints about the palace – and there were many – arose from different perspectives. Some rather grand courtiers felt that even Kensington was too far from their own homes near Whitehall and they resented having to leave the centre of town; others felt it was too ramshackle a house to properly reflect the status of a king. General opinion about the palace was rather like opinion regarding the road to Kensington – some liked it, others hated it.

Take these two reports about the road from Westminster to Kensington. Much of this road still exists today in the form of the famous Rotten Row.

In the first half of the eighteenth century, the Swiss visitor César-François de Saussure wrote in his book *A Foreign View of England in the Reigns of George I and George II*, 'Nothing is more beautiful than the road from … Kensington crossing Hyde Park. It is perfectly straight and so wide that three or four coaches can drive abreast.' He also described the posts along the route 'on the tops of which lanterns are hung and lamps placed in them which are lighted every evening when the Court is at Kensington'.

Yet the diarist and courtier John Hervey, 2nd Baron Hervey (known as Lord Hervey) describes the same road in far less flattering terms in a letter to his mother in 1736:

> The road between this place [Kensington] and London is grown so infamously bad that we live here in the same solitude as we should do if cast on a rock in the middle of the ocean, and all the Londoners tell us there is between them and us a great impassable gulf of mud. There are two roads through the park, but the new one is so convex and the old one so concave, that by this extreme of faults they agree in the common one of being, like the high road, impassable.

Of course, Hervey was writing to entertain his mother and therefore it is probably unwise to assume he was being entirely serious. On the other hand, the discrepancy between the two reports is a reminder that any early description of Kensington Palace and its inhabitants must be taken with a pinch of salt.

Queen Caroline, wife of George II, decided that the problem of the road – which was dusty in summer and muddy in winter – could be solved by making it rather more exclusive. She issued the following decree:

> The king's ministers being very much incommoded by the dustiness of the road leading through Hyde Park, now they are obliged to attend their majesty at Kensington, it was her pleasure that the whole of the said road be kept constantly watered instead of the ring in the park and

that no coaches other than those of the nobility and gentry, be suffered to go into or pass through the park.

A diluted version of this ruling exists today – commercial vehicles are still not allowed down Constitution Hill, or along the Mall to Buckingham Palace beside St James's Park, where Rotten Row originally ran before being shortened in the nineteenth century and effectively ending as it does today at Hyde Park Corner.

But for all its so-called faults, Kensington Palace was a comfortable compromise between a vast and expensive new-build and the distant existing royal residences at Hampton or Windsor. However, William and Mary had always lived in grand surroundings and it is not difficult to believe that for William one of the great attractions of Kensington was not its situation, particularly, nor its gradually completed grand state rooms – it was, in fact, the anemoscope, or wind compass, he had fitted in his gallery at great expense. By the standards of the early eighteenth century it was the ultimate piece of advanced technology. Made by Isaac Thompson, the anemoscope never ceased to delight the king – it allowed him to check the wind direction outside the palace from the comfort of his sofa in the long gallery. Only the very rich could afford an anemoscope. They were usually made by clockmakers using an elaborate series of rods and levers that connected a rooftop weathervane with a long pointer, rather like the minute hand on a clock, fixed on a dial above a mantelpiece. At Kensington the anemoscope 'clock hand' moved across a dial decorated with pictures of the four continents known at that time. A slightly earlier example of a very similar wind compass still exists in the admiralty boardroom at Whitehall. The anemoscope was one of the king's very few concessions to extravagance.

When finally completed around the time of William's death in 1702, Kensington's extensions and remodelling had cost £92,000 – equivalent to roughly £18.5 million in 2018. That sum was only a little less than the cost of the improvements and renovations at Hampton Court that took place at around the same time.

The most impressive rooms at Kensington are still the King's Gallery and the Queen's Gallery and although they were built to show off the monarchs' magnificent collection of pictures, and to inspire awe and admiration in visitors, they also had a more mundane function: they were built to allow the king and queen to walk up and down to exercise on rainy days. Similar long galleries at other houses fulfilled the same function – the long gallery at Jacobean Chastleton House in Oxfordshire, for example, was used for a similar purpose by the children of the Whitmore-Jones family well into the twentieth century.

A great deal of detailed information still exists about who made specific items at Kensington (and how much they cost) in the last years of the seventeenth century and the first years of the eighteenth. Accounts for 1689–91, for example, show that the wainscot and carvings in the Queen's Gallery were made by Henry Hobb and Alexander Frost. The two men also made 'shashes [sashes], shutters, window boards, chimney pieces, picture frames, shelves etc.'.

Other now long-forgotten craftsmen's names are also recorded, and in comes that well-known figure Grinling Gibbons again. Together with Nicholas Alcock, Gibbons carved '1405 feet Ionick medallion and Cornish; 942 feet of picture frame over the door and chimneys and 89 feet of astragal moulding about the glasses in the chimneys'.

Historians tend to use the phrase 'the court' as if it is easily defined. But in this rebuilt palace, what exactly constituted the court? In fact, the court was simply a large group of well-born people who clustered around the king. They were almost always aristocrats, but many were also ministers in the government of the day. All sought the king and visited him as often as possible to discuss business, ask for favours for friends and family or simply to remind him of their existence. He had no choice but to make himself available to them. They were there to persuade him to agree to changes in government policy, or to consult about new appointments to the administration. The court was a curious mix of the social, the political and the commercial. Beautiful people (both male and female) and those with the ability to speak well and wittily often found themselves at the centre of attention and influence, which is why complete strangers might occasionally try to sneak in on the off-chance they would be noticed. There were no security officials at Kensington at that time – if you looked and sounded like a gentleman you might well be admitted to the king's grand rooms, which were often packed with jostling crowds, all hoping they might be lucky.

Many aristocrats attended simply because the king mixed with the great and the good – and aristocrats *were* the great and the good. It was a job, of sorts, simply to be there. Those whose charm and wit – as well as their noble birth – enabled them to get very close to the king and his queen were in many cases able to exert an extraordinary influence. Whoever you were, you were quickly perceived to be either in or out; the sons and daughters of those who had always been at court were automatically admitted, but they might be ignored or snubbed if considered to be dull, boorish or lacking the elegant manners associated with good breeding. Those favoured by the king became in turn the object of flattery and persuasion by those slightly lower in the pecking order, who, if they could not get close enough to the king to lobby on their own behalf, would try the next best thing and lobby the monarch's favourites.

The boorish or unpopular might turn up at Kensington, St James's or Hampton Court only to be snubbed or ignored. Without grace, wit and charm – and good looks – even the greatest aristocrat in the land might struggle to be noticed despite attending the king every day.

According to the historian Lucy Worsley, George II, when Prince of Wales, had a habit of turning his 'rump' on those who were out of favour or whom he disliked – to use the jargon of the day, they had been rumped (a phrase apparently coined by the Earl of Falmouth) and this became almost a badge of honour. Those who had been rumped were allowed to join the Rumpsteak Club, whose existence was a standing joke at the prince's expense. George might rump someone for personal reasons, but usually it was a result of political disagreements – the Earl of Falmouth fell foul of the prince when he ceased to support Sir Robert Walpole's Whig government, for example.

George was apparently furious when he heard about the club and in his thick German accent he asked indignantly if he was being laughed at. Of course, he *was* being laughed at – all the Hanoverians were laughed at. But along with the laughter was a general sense of public gratitude that however laughable they were, the Georges accepted the new dispensation in a way that previous monarchs would not have done.

Official histories tell us that the Georges, like Queen Anne and

William and Mary before them, were, from a political point of view, remarkably good at adapting to the new realities in Britain – to the idea that the British monarch could reign but not rule. So it was not so much how they dealt with the power structures that got them into trouble; it was their personal behaviour, their lives and family relationships.

George II, who continued to live at Kensington and maintain his court there just as William and Mary, Anne and his father George I had done, really would have preferred to stay in Hanover permanently. He almost did so, in fact, spending so much time in Germany that he became immensely unpopular among his British subjects. During one particularly long absence, an anonymous note was attached to the wall of St James's Palace. The note read as follows:

> Lost or strayed out of this house; a man who has left a wife and six children on the Parish; whoever will give tidings of him to the church-wardens of St James's Palace so he may be got again, shall receive four shillings and six pence reward. This reward will not be increased, nobody judging him to deserve a crown.

In the years after the royal family first moved to Kensington, it was Queen Mary who really devoted herself to the palace.

We know that she was personally involved in furnishing her own rooms, for example – and as a result they are far more lavish than those of her husband. She would have known that William, who was far happier on campaign with the army than he ever was at home, cared little for the niceties of interior decoration.

That said, after Mary's death from smallpox in 1694, William's interest in picture collecting seems to have exploded. More than 200 pictures are recorded at Kensington Palace, including more than seventy Old Masters. Many came from the collections of Charles II and James II, and nudes were much in evidence. Many of these pictures proved equally popular with succeeding monarchs, especially George II. On returning from Germany one year he was apoplectic with rage to discover that Queen Caroline had moved his 'large lady' pictures around. He insisted they were put back.

Day-to-day records from William and Mary's time at Kensington are surprisingly detailed when it comes to the vast army of servants underpinning the royals and their court. In *The Secret People of the Palaces*, Joan Glasheen unearths the minutiae of life below stairs at Kensington and other palaces. She provides intriguing lists of William's personal linen, for example; not as grand as the list of his pictures, perhaps, but a wonderfully intimate and revealing detail. Among his possessions we find:

> six pairs of great sheets, four pairs of field-sheets [for use in camp on the battlefield]; 18 day and 18 night shirts; 10 pairs of pillow beres [cases]; 36 laced pocket handkerchiefs; six shaving cloths; four combing cloths; eight dozen napkins; eight dozen stool ducketts; fifteen ivory and fifteen thread buttons.

The stool ducketts, by the way, were reusable cloths for the king's posterior – and they were no doubt proffered at appropriate times by the Groom of the Stole (formerly Groom of the Stool, until around 1660).

At one time the Groom of the Stool would have carried a wooden box with a velvet seat for royal evacuations and really would have helped the monarch clean himself. Instead of a Groom of the Stool, Queen Mary had a 'necessary woman' – Alice Wheeler – to help her, who unlike the Groom of the Stool was not an aristocrat. The queen used a pewter close stool rather than a wooden box.

Whereas William loved pictures, Mary preferred to collect the newly fashionable Chinese and Japanese porcelain and went to great pains to have it magnificently displayed in her private rooms. She had what amounted to a separate court from William – and had to house her numerous attendants, from aristocratic ladies-in-waiting to work-ing-class waiting women, chaplains, personal guards, doctors and letter writers. An interesting aside is that under Anne, who became queen on William's death in 1702, the court employed an official with the wonderful title of Writer and Embellisher of The Queen's Letters to Eastern Princes.

Royal attendants today come from precisely the same high social class as those employed by William and Mary, Anne and the Hanover-ian kings who followed them. Indeed, one or two modern courtiers are direct descendants of seventeenth- and eighteenth-century courtiers. It was – and is, to some extent – a very closed world. The fact that one of Elizabeth II's ancestors may have chopped off the head of one of the Duke of Norfolk's ancestors doesn't matter in the least. Her close friends and advisers are all aristocrats, whether the current Duke of Norfolk, who as Earl Marshall is responsible for state occasions, or

Lord Porchester, for many years the Queen's racing manager and close confidant. In her personal life, Elizabeth II sees the world very much as her ancestors saw it.

So great were the numbers who felt they had a right to be near the king and queen when Kensington Palace established itself as the prime royal residence that nearby Kensington Square (which still retains a few of its original houses) was developed specifically to house them. Among the best-known residents of the square were the maids of honour. Other courtiers lodged at Campden Hill House or Holland House. Mary's sister Anne (later Queen Anne) herself lodged at Holland House for a time during the reign of William and Mary, largely because the royal couple's aforementioned disdain towards Anne's husband, Prince George of Denmark, caused their relationship with her to sour.

Kensington Palace put the village of Kensington on the map and gave it the fashionable aura it retains to this day. For a century and more after William and Mary established their court at Kensington, mansions sprang up along the road towards London, for wherever the king chose to live, the fashionable and well connected were never far behind.

It should be said too that although the court was based at Kensington, it did move – at various times of the year it might be at Whitehall or Windsor, for example. When William returned from the fighting season – which was always the spring and summer – there would be an especially large gathering of courtiers at Kensington.

Balls and public audiences lay at the heart of life at court, but William attended them with very little enjoyment. His distaste for the indulgences of the court did not go unnoticed. He was seen as a dour Calvinist who simply did not know how to have fun. This was almost certainly an oversimplification. We know from a letter written by James Fraser to the Earl of Clarendon – quoted in the splendid *Kensington Palace: Art, Architecture and Society* – that the king did not frown on chocolate drinking, gambling or cards, which were all regularly on offer at balls at Kensington Palace, where five or six hundred people might be present. One can hardly imagine the crush today looking at the state rooms, which though big are not *that* big. We also know that the king loved billiards, especially later in life.

Dining in public was one of those curiosities of the monarch's life – like the king washing the feet of the poor – that had not long died out by the time William was king. The tradition was that the monarch ate with his family, watched by the court, the household staff and any visitors who happened to be about; there might be as many as fifty or sixty spectators, for the monarch was public property. And if dining was a semi-public exercise, in earlier times so too was going to the lavatory. Charles I had to endure the company of his closest advisers, not least, of course, the Groom of the Stool. Elizabeth I refused to be part of this ritual and made sure she had a small lavatorial tent to which she could retreat.

Life at court was like riding an emotional roller-coaster: you might be elated one minute, if the king deigned to speak to you, and despairing the next, if you failed to attract his attention. A select few avoided this because they were always part of the monarch's inner circle. For these lucky individuals there were not only evening entertainments, but also the royal levees at which ministers and the nobility would attend the king as he got out of bed and dressed (*levée* from the French for rising). For a shy, rather private man, which is what in essence William was, the levees, public dining and balls in the evenings must have been a trial at times – perhaps it is no wonder that William preferred to escape to the army each summer.

William's right to the English crown – a right that was not by any means universally accepted – stemmed from his position as the son of Charles I's eldest daughter Mary and also from his Protestantism. It was agreed that he might be king only if he accepted that the age of absolute monarchy had come to an end. The ousted King James II would not have agreed to that.

Invited to take the crown – and who would have turned down such an offer? – William arrived in the West Country with a Dutch army in 1688 and James, realising that he did not have the support of much of the aristocracy, let alone the government, quietly left the country. He was too vain to simply agree to worship privately and discreetly as a Catholic (as Charles II had almost certainly done) and instead insisted that the country must accept him as he was and that he must be allowed to do as he pleased, rather in the manner of Charles I. He simply could not see that the days of English monarchs having unlimited freedom to do what they liked were over. Thus was the Glorious Revolution – glorious in part at least because it was bloodless – effected.

William must have been astonished at the ease of his conquest, if it can be called a conquest. Disillusioned by the clumsy efforts of James II to promote Catholics to prominent positions and by his increasingly autocratic manner, a group of English statesmen effectively invited William to invade. Having received assurances that his 'invasion' would be widely supported, William was happy to oblige. Certainly, his joint rule with his wife Mary (until her death in 1694 and his in 1702) was both stable and relatively uneventful. Mary was William's first cousin and daughter of James II (who had of course been deposed in the Glorious Revolution); she was, conveniently, also Protestant, like her sister Anne, who was to inherit the crown on the death of William in 1702, representing another step away from the old idea of absolute rule, which was supported by many Catholics who believed in the divine right of kings.

William spent a great deal of time abroad, fighting the Jacobites in Ireland and in France, leaving his wife Mary to take her limited turn at running the country. Whenever William returned, Mary discreetly accepted that he was back in charge – even in a royal marriage of joint sovereigns, seventeenth-century wives deferred to their husbands.

As we have seen, Mary delighted in Kensington Palace, but there was always a sense in which it was a halfway house – half rural and half urban, positioned between time spent at Windsor or Hampton Court (the more rural palaces) and Whitehall and St James's, closer to the City.

But if it was a halfway house, it was still a house that defined the point at which the British monarchy had profoundly changed; William and Mary had perhaps chosen Kensington as the focus of their new court precisely because no earlier English monarch had ever done so.

CHAPTER TWO

BUILT FOR SHOW

'In our country, which is governed by money, and where every
man is in pursuit of his own interest, it would be in vain
to look for a real friendship.'

WILLIAM KING

The vast court that moved to Kensington with the monarch always included a few hangers-on who knew that if they looked the part – which meant dressing in expensive clothes so that one looked like a gentleman – they might be admitted to the monarch's private rooms without question. Footmen and other servants would never challenge a man with 'an air of lofty disdain and sufficient lace and silk about his person', as Samuel Johnson was later to put it.

A presumed right of entry was essential even if you happened to have no formal or family connection to the court. Once past the footmen at the door it was more difficult, but if one happened to be noticed by the king or queen, either because of one's looks or because of a sudden demonstration of lightning-fast repartee, one's future at court might be secured. A complete unknown who was regularly witty and entertaining might well be missed if he failed to appear one day. A word from the king would then mean great efforts would be made to persuade the absent person to return to court.

And throughout the reigns of William and Mary and then Anne, work on the palace itself – the setting for the new court – went on, for it was essential that Kensington should continue to impress. Kensington, it might be said, has always been a work in progress. There may have been lengthy periods of neglect, but at other times it has been extensively changed and adapted, leaving only a small number of particularly splendid rooms at its core unaltered.

Creating an impression of regal grandeur became more important for the monarch once real power had been ceded to Parliament; the royal establishment sought to retain the trappings, the aura of influence and power. To this end, William and Mary would have felt compelled to organise the magnificent balls that became a feature of life at Kensington Palace. They were held several times a week throughout much of the year and were in addition to almost daily meetings with ministers and foreign dignitaries; the business of government, which involved advising and being advised by the king, was conducted in the Privy Council room, which was moved to Kensington.

Despite Kensington's rural air, William and Mary actually preferred to be even further away from the city at Hampton Court or Windsor in the summer, but they knew that ministers would object to the long journey on badly made roads or by river, so Kensington kept everyone happy. But the couple's time together at the palace was short – in 1694 Mary contracted smallpox and was dead within a week. William was deeply distressed. For the rest of his life he carried a small lock of her hair and one of her rings in a pouch inside his shirt. William famously died after his horse stumbled on a molehill at Hampton Court in 1702. He broke his collar bone and was taken by carriage back to Kensington Palace, but contracted what was probably pneumonia and died there, much to the delight of Jacobite supporters of the deposed James II. Apart from toasting, to this day, 'the little man in velvet' (the mole that built the molehill!), Jacobites delighted in the fact that the horse William was riding when he fell had been confiscated from the Jacobite Sir John Fenwick. Perhaps the horse, too, had Jacobite sympathies.

The great scandal of William's life was the persistent rumour that he was homosexual. If true, this did not stop Mary becoming pregnant soon after the couple married, but she miscarried and never conceived again. William was unusually close to the young Arnold van Keppel, to whom he gave many of Mary's possessions after she died. Keppel was also made Earl of Albemarle – in fact, he went from pageboy to earl in what has always been seen as a suspiciously short time.

The great diarist Samuel Pepys recorded his impressions of van Keppel. He describes him as a 'blockhead', but van Keppel traded on his looks rather than his brains, and part of the attraction for William was undoubtedly that van Keppel was far younger than him. The consensus today is that William was almost certainly bisexual (he had a mistress, but probably only for form's sake) – although there is another theory which insists that the rumours about William's sexuality were deliberately put about by his enemies, especially the Jacobites. Bisexuality and homosexuality were certainly no strangers to the royal family – James II had his male favourites, as did Edward II. In the case of Edward, one may recall that his relationship with Piers Gaveston was one of the factors that led to him being forced to abdicate in 1327, after which he was almost certainly murdered.

Mary's real love, as we have seen, was her porcelain, and among the wealthy there was a craze for collecting at the end of the seventeenth century. Mary had hundreds of pieces carefully displayed and she was immensely proud of them. The masculine world took a different view, however, as china was seen as 'women's trivia'. When Mary died, much of her china was probably destroyed, although a few pieces survive in the Royal Collection today.

The view that porcelain was considered a woman's affair is aired in John Gay's light-hearted poem 'To a Lady on Her Passion for Old China'.

> What ecstacies her bosom fire!
> How her eyes languish with desire!
> How blest how happy should I be,
> Were that fond glance bestowed on me!
> New doubts and fears within me war,
> What rival's near? A China jar
> China's the passion of her soul;
> A cup, a plate, a dish, a bowl!
> Can kindle wishes in her breast
> Inflame with joy or break her rest…
> Husbands more covetous than sage
> Condemn this China buying rage;

They count that woman's prudence little
Who sets her heart on things so brittle.

There is a playful suggestion that many women preferred their china collections to relationships with people, even their husbands. And this may be true of Mary, who had to accept that William would always be away for much of the year; they were no doubt fond of each other, but the relationship was formal and there is some evidence that William preferred the company of van Keppel, Earl of Albemarle, and of William Bentinck, Earl of Portland, another of his young male favourites.

Had they been able to choose, William and Mary would probably have preferred a semi-retired life. Entertaining was a duty rather than necessarily a pleasure. Family relations were also sometimes difficult to maintain within the narrow confines of Kensington life. In one of her frequently catty letters, Sarah Churchill, Duchess of Marlborough, the great favourite of Queen Anne, reported that Anne and Mary did not get on at all well: 'It was impossible they should be very agreeable companions because Queen Mary grew weary of anyone who would not talk a great deal and the princess [Anne] was so silent that she rarely spoke more than was necessary to answer a question.' William and Mary's attitude to Anne's husband made things even worse. But it wasn't only William and Mary who tended to disparage Prince George of Denmark. Charles II, Anne's uncle, said of George, 'I have tried him drunk and I have tried him sober and there is nothing in him.'

Despite her desire to defend and promote her husband, Anne's greatest passion was for the Duchess of Marlborough. Their relationship lives on in the thousands of letters Sarah wrote to the queen that are preserved today in the British Library. Anne's private dining room at Kensington Palace, surprisingly small and wonderfully mellowed with age – a room where almost all of the two women's intimacies took place – still looks today as it did in the first decade of the eighteenth century and is among the state rooms that can be visited by the public.

Charles II's characterisation of Prince George may have been wide of the mark – he was certainly no great judge of character, preferring the company of notorious men such as John Wilmot, Earl of Rochester: a brilliant poet but also a dangerous, promiscuous and highly unreliable individual.

Queen Anne may or may not have had a physical relationship with the Duchess of Marlborough – the evidence is inconclusive at best – but they certainly had an intense connection, and that intensity is reflected in the vast number of letters they wrote to each other using pseudonyms; Sarah was Mrs Freeman and Anne Mrs Morley. But the letters, mostly written from Kensington to Sarah at Woodstock in Oxfordshire, had as much to do with power as friendship. Anne loved what she saw as Sarah's honesty, frequently accepting her advice on matters of state, but having the power to say what she really felt seems to have gone to Sarah's head and a relationship based on honest advice seems to have become one that was periodically bullying and insensitive.

Monarchs have always claimed to hate flatterers, perhaps because they are usually surrounded by them. But Sarah Churchill – who had been friends with Anne since childhood – allowed familiarity to breed a certain element of contempt. She frequently overstepped the mark and spoke to Anne as if she were the village idiot. Eventually Anne could stand it no longer; she dismissed Sarah and never spoke to her again.

During their happy years, the correspondence between Anne and Sarah was remarkable in many ways – not least for its suggestion of real affection – but it has been seen in more recent times as evidence of a sexual liaison. That assumption is based perhaps on the idea that this particular intimate relationship between two women was unique, or nearly so. In fact, as the historian Keith Thomas points out in his masterly book *The Ends of Life*, relationships such as that between Sarah and Anne were fairly common among upper-class women in seventeenth- and eighteenth-century England. Part of the fun of the game of writing to each other was precisely the fact that false names were used, no doubt adding to the sense of secret intimacy.

Thomas explains the background to such relationships:

In the 1650s the poet Katherine Philips (the 'matchless Orinda') who, at the age of sixteen had been married to a Welsh gentleman of fifty-four, formed a much-imitated Society of Friendship. Animated by doctrines of platonic love introduced from France, strongly Royalist in sympathy, and linked by correspondence rather than personal encounters, this group was virtual rather than actual. Its members followed the precise affectation of giving each other names from contemporary romances: Orinda's friends included Ardelia, Palaemon, Lucasia and Silvander. Although her society initially included men as well as women, what mattered most to Philips was female friendship, which she celebrated in numerous poems as,

Nobler than kindred or marriage band
Because more free.

Like many other seventeenth- and eighteenth-century women, Anne believed that relationships between females were preferable to the inequalities of marriage and did more for female development. As the poet Mary Chandler would write in 1733:

> Friendship's the sweetest joy of human life
> 'tis that I wish, and not to be a wife.

It is very much in this light that we should view the relationship and correspondence between Mrs Freeman and Mrs Morley.

Anne's greatest physical legacy at Kensington is the Orangery – or, as she described it, the greenhouse.

Unlike the house itself – a mix of styles and periods – the Orangery is all of a piece: balanced in proportion and therefore beloved of architects and architectural historians. The outside remains much today as playwright and architect Sir John Vanbrugh (with a little help, almost certainly, from Christopher Wren and Nicholas Hawksmoor) designed it, but of course it has not been venerated by every generation – its interior was hacked about mercilessly by succeeding generations until well into the twentieth century. All are agreed, however, that it is a fine example of the English baroque. What is a little more interesting is that the builders employed by Vanbrugh turned out to be thugs who almost got into a punch-up with each other!

The man who was supposed to supervise the building was one Ben Jackson, but according to rules laid down by the Office of Works, to avoid any accusations of corruption Mr Jackson could not also carry out the building work. Vanbrugh therefore offered the work to a shadowy Mr Hill, only to discover that this man quickly disappeared when threatened with a beating by Jackson's men. Wren and Vanbrugh may even have been a little afraid of these tough workmen themselves, for when they discovered that Jackson had got round the rules by arranging for his deputy to submit bills in his name, the two great architects did nothing except fume at someone they considered a crook.

Whatever Mr Jackson's moral failings, he made a splendid job of the Orangery, to the delight of Queen Anne.

One curious use to which the Orangery has been put – and it has been many things, from gambling room to garden shed – was as a setting for the ceremony of touching for the king's evil. The disease referred to is scrofula, a condition that causes the lymph nodes to swell. Anne revived this tradition – William had refused to do it (he'd also refused to take part in the tradition that involved the monarch washing the feet of the poor), much to the disgust of his subjects, so Anne, no doubt with an eye to increasing her popularity, did it at the Orangery. The ceremony was an ancient one, but there was some disagreement over whether a woman, however anointed, could or should do it. Much to her credit, Queen Anne took no notice of her critics and over the following years 'touched' thousands of her grateful subjects.

In his *Life of Samuel Johnson* James Boswell records how his great protagonist's parents took advantage of this development:

His mother ... carried him to London, where he was actually touched by Queen Anne. Mrs Johnson indeed, as Mr Hector informed me, acted by the advice of the celebrated Sir John Floyer, then a physician in

Lichfield. Johnson used to talk of this very frankly; and Mrs Piozzi has preserved his very picturesque description of the scene, as it remained upon his fancy. Being asked if he could remember Queen Anne, 'He had (he said) a confused, but somehow a sort of solemn recollection of a lady in diamonds, and a long black hood.' This touch, however, was without any effect. I ventured to say to him, in allusion to the political principles in which he was educated, and of which he ever retained some odour, that 'his mother had not carried him far enough; she should have taken him to ROME.' [i.e. to the Old Pretender]

While her public life continued its steady course, Anne's relationship with Sarah, Duchess of Marlborough, was becoming ever more complex. King William had hated the fact that his wife's sister was so close to Sarah because Sarah's husband, though a brilliant soldier, was considered too much of a maverick to be fully trusted.

That said, Anne and William seemed to have got on better after Mary's death, perhaps because Anne accepted some of the burden of duties normally undertaken by the consort. But nothing could transform William into a witty or entertaining king in the manner of the 'Merry Monarch', his uncle Charles II.

The historical record may portray William unfairly (in part because there isn't much of it), but as Bryan Bevan notes in his book *King William*, a comment made by the Countess of Rutland might give an idea of the general feeling about him. The countess was at Kensington Palace one evening in 1701 when William attempted to walk past her through a narrow gap in the crowd. She noticed a footstool in the king's way and went to move it aside. 'It is no matter,' he apparently said, and stepped over the stool. The Countess of Rutland thought this an example of the king's great charm and easy manners, but one suspects her comment was heavily ironic.

The truth is we know very little of William in the domestic sphere, but we do know he was keen to polish his public persona. He made a point of saying he used public money for the defence of the nation rather than on 'sumptuous palaces' – hence the relatively modest work at Kensington Palace, at least compared to the excesses of other European rulers. Upon succeeding William as monarch, Anne was sometimes seen to exercise similar restraint with the nation's money – she had some old cabinets dismantled and remade into tables for her rooms at Kensington; she also cut down and altered a magnificent writing desk, which is still in the Royal Collection. George I was not to be quite so careful: in 1724 he ordered £5,000 worth of new furniture for Kensington Palace, including chairs for himself and stools for his courtiers. The stools at least were something of an irrelevance, as in the large reception rooms at Kensington and his other palaces, chairs were not generally needed as no one was allowed to sit in the presence of the king.

Anne's desire to be frugal may have impressed Parliament, but it made the English aristocracy look down on William, who, despite his Stuart ancestry, was seen as foreign; he did not understand the 'right way' to live, which meant living in as grand a manner as possible – or at least that was the view of a number of English earls.

Perhaps the memory of Charles II led people to expect more from both William and Anne as respective monarchs. There is a sense that they both lived too quietly at Kensington. Anne Somerset in her book *Queen Anne* quotes a young visitor to Kensington Palace who called upon Queen Anne when she was ill and reported afterwards that 'her palace at Kensington where she commonly resided was a perfect solitude. Few houses in England belonging to persons of quality were kept in a more private way.' Another visitor, again quoted by Anne Somerset, said, 'There is nothing but ceremony; no manner of conversation.'

But Anne tried hard for William after Mary's death and in the summer of 1699 she agreed at the request of the Earl of Albemarle (the king's handsome young favourite) to host a weekly reception where gambling and music were on offer. The idea, according to Anne Somerset, was that the court would associate these pleasures with William and cease to think of him as too quiet and rather a bore.

The first reception was an abject failure because neither William nor Anne realised that to make the event successful, alcohol was essential – the following week it was added to the mix and the receptions went swimmingly thereafter. William took the credit for his improved reputation.

But if William was able to adapt to the needs and expectations of his new role as sole monarch, he was not quite as ready or able to alter some of his rather petty private habits. He was, for example, notoriously greedy. The Duchess of Marlborough (by no means an objective witness, it must be admitted) recalled how when a small dish of new green peas was placed on the table before the king and various nobles – not to mention Anne – he snatched the plate without a word and ate every last pea.

The Dukes of Marlborough down to this day have Sarah Churchill to thank for their luck in being given the estate at Blenheim in Oxfordshire that remains theirs today. Anne gave it to Sarah when their relationship was at its best. William might not have been so generous, and by the time the duchess and the queen fell out, Anne would no doubt have loved to take the gift back if she had been able.

The eventual break with Sarah was made easier for Anne, who always needed an intimate companion, by the arrival of Abigail Masham. Abigail offered all the comfort and intimacy of Sarah's relationship with the queen but without the increasing abruptness and desire for control. The great irony is that Sarah introduced Abigail (an impoverished relation) into the royal household in the first place. In addition to her increasing impatience with the queen, Sarah also seems to have been something of a thief. On one occasion she helped herself to £12,000 from the Privy Purse without permission. The queen, with her new favourite solidly behind her, eventually felt strong enough to dismiss Sarah. During their final encounter Sarah seems to have completely lost control – she cried and screamed that Abigail Masham and the Duke and Duchess of Somerset and others had been blackening her name. The queen turned her back on Sarah and said nothing.

But Sarah could not be thrown out quite yet, as the queen knew her former favourite had kept a large number of compromising letters from 'Mrs Morley'. Knowing she was still in a position of power, Sarah took another £21,000 from the Privy Purse without permission and then a final £18,000. Sarah judged that the queen would keep quiet lest her letters be revealed. And how would it look if the queen accused Sarah of stealing from the Privy Purse when she, Anne, had made Sarah Keeper of the Privy Purse, not to mention Groom of the Stool, Mistress of the Robes and Ranger of Windsor Great Park? On the other hand, the amounts taken without the queen's permission were colossal and this was done at a time when a commoner might easily be hanged for stealing a bedsheet; the maid Catherine Pollard, who worked at Kensington for decades, was hanged after stealing a few silver plates, for example. But there were amusing moments in the slow decline of the two women's relationship. Historian Ernest Law explains how, during one dispute, Sarah and Anne nearly came to blows, 'but being women and conscious of the need to be decorous in everything, they began to try to push each other out of the room' – inevitably, as Law points out, 'Anne's sheer bulk won the day'.

Once she had ousted Sarah, Anne made sure Abigail Masham was given all the prerequisites of her new status as royal favourite. She was given a large suite of rooms at Kensington and according to Joan Glasheen they were richly furnished. Surviving inventories list, among other items, 'two large cushions for our dog, five pieces of in-grain silk lacing being for window curtains and forty-one ounces of crimson, green and white silk tufted fringe with crepe for Mrs Masham's lodging'.

Writing at the turn of the nineteenth century, Ernest Law reminds us that when Anne died at Kensington in 1714 she was a sad and lonely figure despite the attentions of Abigail. One reasonably plausible theory is that, like the Duchess of Marlborough, Abigail – who was five years younger than Anne – represented a chance for the queen to create the sort of relationship she might have had with her children had any of them lived. Beyond Abigail, her greatest comfort in her final years seems to have been food and especially chocolate. Roger Coke confirms this:

Her life would have lasted longer if she had not eaten so much … she supped too much chocolate and died monstrously fat; insomuch that the coffin wherein her remains were deposited was almost square and was bigger than that of her husband the prince who was known to be a fat bulky man.

But at least Anne's coffin – unlike that of her sister Mary – did not damage the magnificent carved staircase when it was carried out of the palace.

If, as Ernest Law claims, William and Mary enjoyed living at Kensington, Anne absolutely adored it, but most especially the garden. William and Mary had created a garden of clipped hedges, gravelled paths and statues and urns – the standard, highly ordered model for gardens of the period. Accounts from this time record, 'To Edward Pearce for carving a chair for the garden [at Kensington] with a canopy of drapery, £43.16 shillings; for carving more chairs and two seats with dolphins, scallop shells etc and other works done about the said gardens £42. 2s 4d.' None of these chairs and statues – nor indeed the seventeenth-century formal gardens – remain today.

Most of the parterres and formal walkways were to be swept away by Queen Caroline, wife of George II, who certainly preferred the garden to the house. But Anne was an enthusiastic gardener who undoubtedly made her mark at Kensington. Writing in *Antiquities of Middlesex*, published in 1705, John Bowack explains:

> There is a noble collection of foreign plants and fine, neat greens which makes it [Kensington] pleasant all the year and the contrivance, variety and disposition of the whole is extremely pleasing … the whole not being above twenty six acres. Her majesty has been pleased to plant nearly thirty acres more towards the north and separated from the rest by a stately green house.

Writing in 1711 in *The Spectator*, Joseph Addison notes that the upper garden at Kensington near what was then called the Acton Road (now the Bayswater Road) was once 'nothing but gravel pits'. But thanks to Queen Anne that had all changed: 'It must have been a fine genius for gardening that could have thought of transforming such an unsightly hollow into so beautiful an area.'

Kensington Gardens is roughly the same size now as it was in the early 1700s, although around 100 acres were taken from Hyde Park and added to the Kensington estate at the request of Queen Anne, who wanted to create a deer paddock. The Hyde Park ranger was given £200 to compensate for the loss.

Kensington Gardens had its own entirely separate park keeper, and this had to be a nobleman as it was a sinecure traditionally offered to a specially favoured courtier or royal servant. William gave the job to his favourite (and possibly lover) William Bentinck, Earl of Portland. The earl had to have a grand title in addition to the money; he was made 'Superintendent of their Majesties' Gardens and Plantations within the Boundary Lines of Their Majesties' said house at Kensington'.

CHAPTER THREE

SERVANTS, COURTIERS
AND HANGERS-ON

'A court is an assemblage of noble and distinguished beggars.'
CHARLES-MAURICE DE TALLEYRAND-PÉRIGORD

*'Practise in everything a certain nonchalance that shall conceal
design and show that what is done and said is done without
effort and almost without thought.'*
BALDASSARE CASTIGLIONE, *THE BOOK OF THE COURTIER*

The history of the court – that vague amorphous cloud of people that traditionally surrounded the monarch – is curious, and especially so when it relates to Kensington, which always seemed to be part house and part palace, given its bucolic location and relatively modest size.

Many court traditions began at Whitehall Palace, that rambling shambolic swathe of ancient and modern houses and halls running from Parliament Square to what is now Trafalgar Square. Foreign visitors were frequently astonished at the ramshackle nature of the palace, which differed so markedly from the sort of palaces in which European monarchs lived.

At Whitehall it wasn't just the buildings themselves that seemed so haphazard – for those buildings were connected to each other by hundreds of alleyways, tunnels, covered passageways and courtyards. Foreign dignitaries were terrified of losing their way in this extraordinary village.

At Whitehall, whether indoors or out, the monarch was accompanied by his courtiers and by petitioners, curious passers-by, servants and anyone else who had the time to stop and stare. They watched while he walked in Whitehall Gardens, while he ate with his family and, as we have seen, when he went to the lavatory. Virtually anyone suitably dressed could walk on the outer edge of the throng, for there were no gates or security staff. The penalty for any attempt on the king's life was so terrifying that it was simply assumed that no one would dare make such an attempt.

But accompanying the king at a relative distance was a very different matter from being part of his select and intimate circle. This kind of unfettered access to the monarch seems to have diminished proportionally as the monarch's power lessened and although, as we have seen, the audacious might still bluff their way into the king's levee at Kensington, both William and Mary and later Anne created a sense of almost middle-class reticence and privacy at Kensington that did not exist during the reign of Charles II and earlier monarchs. But an element of the hectic nature of Whitehall Palace did pervade Kensington and it was linked to the sense that the monarch must be seen by the people.

As Adrian Tinniswood notes in his book *Behind the Throne*, 'For most of its history the royal household gave an impression of barely controlled chaos.' This chaos included strangers wandering into the buildings at Whitehall and staying perhaps for years – even finding rooms that were unoccupied and moving in. Part of the problem was that servants were there in such huge numbers that it was difficult if not impossible to keep tabs on them. There was no written record, no staff ledger in which such information might be recorded. And servants were perfectly at liberty to arrange for their relatives to deputise for them, sometimes for months at a time. All the servants ate at the king's expense and it was impossible to check who had a right to eat and who did not.

As late as the mid-twentieth century, similar situations still arose. In a recent biography of the Queen Mother's favourite servant, William Tallon, we read that:

The day-to-day practical duties of the below-stairs world at Buckingham Palace were enlivened by gossip and there were always rumours about the royals, especially the minor members of the family, and the royal hangers-on. Billy [William Tallon] later recalled 'one old lunatic' who was always at Buckingham Palace but no one – certainly not the servants – had a clue who he was or why he was there. Rumour had it that he was a retired butler, now in his eighties, but no one seemed able to remember. The royal family let it be known that the old man was not to be questioned or hindered in any way. As a fellow servant recalled:

'Every January he was reputed to give up smoking and drinking and to walk around with half a raw cabbage in his pocket. Whenever he was hungry, he would whip out the cabbage and take a bite. He was very eccentric, but was more or less part of the furniture! No one questioned his right to be there.'

The greatest difficulty with the court, whether at Whitehall, Buckingham Palace or Kensington, was that in addition to the huge number of royal servants, there were also countless servants working for the various courtiers. A very grand courtier might have almost as many servants as the king himself. No aristocrat worth his salt would dream of having fewer servants than he felt his status required. In addition to these two tiers of servants – those of the royal family and those of the courtiers – there were senior servants who, in turn, had their own domestic staff.

For servants, the line between what they were entitled to and what they might take without risk of punishment was always blurred. Servants always stole if they could get away with it and they were paid a pittance precisely because it was assumed that they would steal. Even at the coronation of a king, food, cutlery, glasses, bunting and even the tables on which the feast had been served would all be pilfered at the end of the day.

This kind of thing was always at its worst at the royal palaces. At St James's, for example, a royal servant – Mr Fortnum – did such a good job stealing candle ends and other small but useful items that in 1707, he was able to go into business with his landlord, Mr Mason. They set up a shop just up the road from the palace. The shop was successful; Mr Fortnum left royal service and the two men made their fortunes in the famous department store that bears their name to this day.

The pandemonium of the royal household extended further, to matters of hygiene and sanitation. The great and the good as well as their servants all urinated in the palace wherever they happened to be – if the king happened to be playing cards, he might simply walk into the corner of the room and relieve himself if he couldn't be bothered to walk any distance to a closet. Even at Kensington there were only buckets or commodes, often tucked away in tiny cavities behind the fireplaces.

As Adrian Tinniswood notes in *Behind the Throne*, the problem became so bad that at Whitehall, St James's and Kensington, 'No pissing' signs were nailed up at key locations. It was the sheer numbers of people involved that caused the problem, not the simple fact of public urination. We must bear in mind that this was a time when hardly anyone bathed regularly and neither soap nor deodorant had been invented. People generally would have been far more tolerant of unpleasant smells than we are today, so those 'No pissing' signs suggest that the problem was exceptionally acute.

The odd thing about courtiers is that other than accompanying the king and begging favours for their friends, it is difficult to know why they were there, other than because it gave them something to do. For ministers, of course, it was different, although they were almost invariably aristocrats too. They had the business of government to discuss, but the other senior members of the court merely buzzed around the monarch trying to amuse him (or her) and each other. They were simply filling their time in a manner considered in keeping with their status. Class divisions at Kensington, as elsewhere, were rigid. Ladies-in-waiting (and for the king, gentlemen-in-waiting) were always from the nobility and their roles were largely limited to simply being in attendance; lower-class women and men did the real work of cleaning, washing, cooking, changing beds, lighting fires and laying the tables.

But however aristocratic the gentlemen- and ladies-in-waiting were, they were not considered quite good enough to marry into the monarchy. Until very recent times, the British royal family insisted on looking to Germany to find suitable marriage partners for their children. When it came to the marriages of most of her children, even Queen Victoria thought minor German princes to be more suitable, in the main, than English aristocrats. A prince or princess from an impoverished German state the size of the Isle of Wight was almost always preferable to the son or daughter of an English duke because of the obsession with titles, even when the origin of those titles was dubious to say the least. Keeping marriage within these exceptionally narrow bands was due, of course, to the now utterly discredited idea of blood purity – a notion that to some extent survived even the discovery that marrying one's close relatives could lead to serious genetic disabilities: enormous chins (a medical condition known as mandibular prognathism) for the Hapsburgs, for example, and haemophilia for the British and Russian royal families.

Of course, the system of privilege that surrounds courtiers and the nobility survives to this day and for some it represents the last vestige of 'old corruption'. Kensington Palace has frequently been at the centre of public disagreements focusing on these issues. A major row broke out in the early 2000s, for example, when the press discovered that Prince and Princess Michael of Kent were living virtually rent-free at Kensington Palace. The row was reminiscent of the furious debates that took place over the spending of the Prince Regent in the early nineteenth century. The Kents eventually agreed to pay a market rent for their residence but grace-and-favour apartments still exist at Kensington, Hampton Court and elsewhere. In many ways the system has not changed much at all since William and Mary's reign.

Then again, the royal family has always been slow to react to changes in public opinion and seems to have found discussions of public spending distasteful. Despite being under pressure from Parliament to reduce household expenditure, Queen Victoria was outraged, for example, when it was suggested that the role of Hereditary Grand Falconer should be abolished. Parliament had been paying £1,200 a year to an obscure relative of the queen's for this role, but there was a snag – the queen did not own, nor had she ever owned, a single falcon.

Inevitably the queen got her way and her relative continued to be paid for doing nothing other than sitting with the queen occasionally and amusing her.

Senior servants, whether Groom of the Stool or Keeper of Windsor Great Park, were not expected to work and that tradition has continued right up to the present. Other servants further down the ladder do the real work today, just as they did more than two centuries ago.

During William Tallon's working life he was expected to work ten or twelve hours at a stretch, for six or sometimes seven days a week, for a salary that would amount to perhaps 10 per cent of that paid to an equerry. By contrast, the vaguely aristocratic Alan 'Tommy' Lascelles was not only given a Rolls-Royce by the queen when he retired; he was also allowed to live rent-free for the rest of his life in the recently rebuilt stables at Kensington Palace. William Tallon was exiled to a council flat in south London on *his* retirement.

There was, however, a price to pay for privilege and for Lascelles it was a price paid over many years at Kensington Palace. As private secretary to the queen he had been a key figure in preventing Princess Margaret from marrying Group Captain Peter Townsend in the 1950s. When Margaret married Antony Armstrong-Jones instead – a marriage that was doomed from the outset – the couple went to live at Kensington. Unfortunately, Lascelles also lived at the palace and for nearly twenty years (until Lascelles's death in 1981) Margaret ignored or avoided Lascelles; she certainly never spoke a civil word to him and one servant insisted she actually spat as she passed him if she could not avoid crossing his path. It was common knowledge that she hated Lascelles.

But Lascelles was exactly the sort of courtier one might have found at the court at Kensington in the eighteenth century or earlier. He despised both Townsend and Armstrong-Jones as commoners and believed that the royal family should marry only into other royal houses.

Courtiers today almost invariably come from the same aristocratic families that have always been associated with the royals, but in the past and especially at Kensington the same thing was true of servants lower down the social scale. Particular names crop up again and again through the generations. Joan Glasheen has skilfully tracked a number of families whose serving roles were handed down to sons and daughters, grandsons and granddaughters.

Simon de Brienne, for example, started his working life as William III's barber. By 1691 he had been promoted to housekeeper at Kensington Palace. His wife Mary became keeper of the standing wardrobe at Kensington; their joint salary was £300, a considerable sum for the seventeenth century when one considers that, even allowing for inflation, a maid in 1920s London was likely to be earning just £50 a year.

Other servants might shift between very different jobs – Charles

Bland went from being William's Page of the Robes to 'weigher of the gold and silver'. Odd shifts from one job to another entirely unrelated job might occur within one generation, as with the Briennes, or across one generation to the next – but, like carpenters and shoemakers, servants and courtiers followed in their parents' footsteps.

Many jobs seem to have been created merely to ensure that there were lots of servants around. The list of royal servants in the early eighteenth century includes, for example, 'the laundress to the body, the semptress, the keeper of the fowl; the rat killer and mole taker'. In 1689 a new post was created when Robert Moss was employed to 'Attend All the Affairs of the Printing Press For the Better Discovering and Suppressing all Scandalous and Unlicensed Books By Pamphleteers'.

By the time George II ascended the throne, the job of rat killer at Kensington, as mentioned by Joan Glasheen, had been offered to a woman – Elizabeth Stubbs – and by 1815 another woman, Mary Longley, had taken over as live-in chimney sweep at Kensington.

No sooner had these various people started work – whether aristocrats attached to the monarch's person or lowlier servants – than they began to lobby for jobs for their friends or family members. It was just the way things were done. And the situation was complicated, as we have seen, by the fact that aristocratic staff of the royal household had their own servants, who in turn had *their* own servants.

By the time of William and Mary, and subsequently through the eighteenth century, there were increasing attempts to at least keep lists of servants at the royal palaces, but they were not systematically maintained and many earlier practices continued long after they had officially been brought to an end. Just as the well dressed and confident could still bluff their way into the king's presence at Kensington, so too could the friends of servants bluff their way into the kitchens for lunch or dinner.

Perhaps the most striking example of family continuity among senior servants is that of the Keppels. As late as 1944, more than two centuries after William seems to have fallen in love with Arnold van Keppel, there was still a Keppel in the royal household. This was Sir Derek Keppel, Master of the Household. A slightly earlier Keppel, who worked for Edward VII, was married to Edward's favourite mistress. In return for his acquiescence in the affair, this Keppel was given a lucrative position at court. All the Keppels grew rich on their royal connections.

Servants at the lower end of the scale often also became rich – Jane Keen, the housekeeper at Kensington Palace during the 1840s and 1850s, is said to have retired with more than £2,000 in the bank. An astonishing figure for the time – perhaps equivalent to £250,000 today. Much of this money would have come from bribes – the housekeeper would take money in return for agreeing to find a job for someone or for putting in a good word for a tradesman or even for allowing visitors into the palace when the king was absent.

And less senior servants really did still have power. They were courted by outsiders – not to the extent that aristocratic servants were, of course, but there were still parallels. Samuel Pepys occasionally lunched with royal servants, for example, recording that William Chaffinch (of the Chaffinchs who worked at various royal palaces for three generations) had shown him the king's private apartments: 'Mr Cheffinch [sic] being by did take us of his own accord into the king's closet which indeed is a very noble place; a great variety of pictures. I could have spent three hours there.'

Joan Glasheen expertly traces the Chaffinch family from the time of Charles II well into the eighteenth century. Charles employed Thomas Chaffinch (or Cheffinch, the spelling varies) as Page of the Bedchamber; his wife Dorothy was Laundress to the Body. The Chaffinchs' daughter Mary became laundress to Queen Catherine, while Thomas's younger brother William became Groom of Her Majesty's Privy Chamber. William's reputation was none too savoury; an anonymous versifier wrote of him:

> It happened in the twilight of the day
> As England's monarch in his closet lay
> And Chiffinch stepped to fetch the female prey.

The Count de Grammont (1621–1707) also knew Chaffinch and described him as 'a notorious pander to Charles II'.

William Chaffinch later became Page of the Backstairs (a role performed by William Tallon in the twentieth century) and Keeper of Hyde Park, eventually retiring with a splendid pension of £200 a year. But perhaps the greatest longevity among servants can be found in the career of Percy Kirke, who worked for fifty years for no fewer than four monarchs starting with Charles II.

❦

The great allure of life at court, then and now, is the attraction of power – as well as the chance to get rich for doing little, if you are a younger son from an aristocratic family. The sad thing is that servants at the bottom of the chain of command no longer have the chance to become rich like Jane Keen or hugely influential like William and Thomas Chaffinch. Their hours and pay may now be regulated by law, but they have almost no chance of being noticed and rewarded on the whim of the monarch. In the eighteenth century, especially at Kensington Palace, a favoured servant might very occasionally be more influential than a courtier. He might be despised by the nobility, but even the nobles knew that to gain access to George I, for example, it was essential, as we will see, to be on good terms with two of the most remarkable servants in the history of the British royal family: they were Mohammed and Mustapha, so-called 'servants of the body'.

The division between equerries and other grandee titles is, as we have seen, unashamedly class-based. Lord Alrincham (1924–2001) was absolutely right when he told Queen Elizabeth II that it was a mistake to surround herself with 'tweedy types', but his advice has largely gone unheeded. Royal snobbery in this regard is just a fact of life. Even girlfriends (who were destined to remain only girlfriends) of royals were sneered at well into the twentieth century. George V refused to call one of his son's girlfriends, Freda Dudley Ward, by name and instead referred to her only as 'the lace-maker's daughter'. Her family had a trade background and he was horrified. When Princess Margaret married Antony Armstrong-Jones and moved into Kensington Palace with him, the household was aghast. Armstrong-Jones was the son of a barrister and therefore an upstart. The senior staff looked down on him, insisting on referring to him as 'the Welshman' or 'Mr Armstrong-Jones' even after he was ennobled by the Queen as Lord

Snowdon. The irony, as one former servant explained, is that within a few years of his marriage, Armstrong-Jones had become far more of a snob than his wife, the Queen's sister.

> He spoke to us as if he was the king himself and wasn't in the least both-ered about asking us to do little jobs that would have taken him three seconds. He enjoyed ringing the servants' bell, as it were – he came to believe that he was a very important person. He even spoke to Margaret as if she was less important than he was. She was furious and would refer to him, when he was in the room with her and she was talking to a friend, as 'that grubby little Welshman'.

Perhaps because of the failure of her sister's marriage, Elizabeth II rec-ognised, in allowing the marriage of Prince William to the commoner Catherine Middleton, that the old ways are not always the best. The old ways destroyed the happiness of Princess Margaret and she spent decades at Kensington Palace licking her wounds. Now William and Kate live at Kensington in a manner that Margaret would perhaps have envied. Not only that but William and Kate live in the very same apartment that Princess Margaret and her husband once made their home – although 'apartment' is an absurd word for what is effectively a four-storey house, taking up half a large area of the palace never open to the public known as Clock Court.

But the seductive charms of admittance to the royal family – either as servant, courtier or newlywed – are legion, and what begins as a fairy tale can end, as it did for Margaret and for the late Diana, Princess of Wales, as a nightmare.

A number of people who work at the palace have confirmed that though Catherine Middleton seems remarkably immune so far to the poisonous aspects of life as part of 'the Firm', Meghan Markle, the most recent arrival at Kensington Palace, has not been so lucky. As we will see, the presence of the newest royals – symbols of a modern egalitarianism in the royal family – has led the monarchy away from the old squabbles about precedence and blood relationships, but perhaps into new and perhaps even more difficult territory. In this new territory the mere fact of being royal is no longer enough; royals must seem royal but also have far more of the common touch than they were ever expected to have in the past. Suddenly finding oneself part of the royal family can have an absurd inflationary effect on the ego.

The politician Sir Henry 'Chips' Channon summed this up nicely when he said of Wallis Simpson, long before she married Edward VIII, 'She already walks into a room as if she … expected to be curtsied to.'

Social power, it seems, corrupts as much as political and economic power.

CHAPTER FOUR

THOSE MAD GEORGIANS

'George the First was always reckoned
Vile, but viler still the Second,
And what mortal ever heard,
Any good of George the Third.
When from earth the Fourth descended,
God be praised, the Georges ended.'

ANON

Members of the royal family and their servants, courtiers and hangers-on in general may frequently be mad, bad and dangerous to know, but it is difficult now to comprehend the endless lunacies of the Hanoverians. After Queen Anne died without an heir in 1714, the British crown was offered to George I, Elector of Hanover, Anne's nearest Protestant relative, as the Act of Settlement of 1701 had stipulated.

An extraordinary number of Catholics – more than fifty in fact – had a far greater right to the crown than George, at least according to the rules of primogeniture, and despite the fact that many close relatives of earlier Stuart monarchs later became Protestants. Britain, for good or ill, found itself looking up to the first in a series of rather small, bad-tempered Germans.

Many historians insist that George I was a good constitutional monarch. He was certainly no worse than many kings, but perhaps rather unforgiving – he famously arranged, for example, to have his wife's lover murdered. Long before he was offered the crown of England, he had married the young Sophia Dorothea of Brunswick-Lüneburg-Celle (1666–1726). The marriage was arranged and Sophia's slightly inferior origins were overlooked on the grounds that she had money (and George needed money). When she was first told that she was to marry George, she apparently screamed that she would not under any circumstances marry 'the pig snout'. She must have sensed they were remarkably ill-suited – she was beautiful, light-hearted and enjoyed parties and balls and having fun. George, by contrast, was taciturn, even morose; he was short, slightly dumpy and both uninterested and uninteresting. Had he not been king, the courtiers who bowed and scraped before him when he eventually came to England would have despised him – he had none of those qualities that courtiers most admired. He was not witty or amusing; he was not engagingly polite or even a reasonable conversationalist. He was what the great memoirist of the Hanoverians John Hervey would have called a 'dullard'.

Samuel Johnson said of him, 'George I knew nothing and desired to know nothing; did nothing and desired to do nothing.'

His alliance with the bubbly, fun-loving and by all accounts witty Sophia was bound to come to grief. In fact, the marriage foundered remarkably quickly. George had always had mistresses, but it was a slightly different matter when his own wife became the mistress of the Swedish Count Philip Christoph von Königsmark.

George might have been able to forgive this if Sophia had chosen to be discreet. From the start of the marriage he had made it clear that he much preferred his exceedingly thin mistress (with whom he was to have three daughters) Melusine von der Schulenburg (1667–1743). But when word got out that Sophia and von Königsmark were planning to elope – in other words, when it became clear that Sophia was no longer prepared to conduct her liaison discreetly – George's family arranged, rather like the Mafia, the disappearance of the Swedish count. According to historians he was either killed and thrown into a river or killed and then chopped into pieces and buried beneath the floorboards of George's castle in Hanover.

Of course, there is no definitive proof that George was behind any of this, but we do know that Königsmark vanished for ever, and had the case arisen today George would almost certainly have been convicted of murder under the joint enterprise rules. Sophia wasn't killed – instead she was locked in a castle and allowed to see no one, not even her children. She stayed in her castle, living in luxury but unable to leave, for the next thirty years. She died without ever having seen her son again.

George may have been rather ruthless, but all this happened long before he arrived in England in 1714. He had accepted the crown of Great Britain and Ireland, but it was something that all his subsequent behaviour suggested he didn't really want. For the rest of his life he returned as often as he could to Hanover; indeed, he was absent for roughly half the summers of his total reign; he never learned to speak English fluently, despised his new home and would have retired completely from public life if he could – what probably stopped him was that his far more outgoing son, George, the Prince of Wales (later George II), set up a rival court in London that began to attract the great and the good of England.

The fact that the Prince of Wales had, as it were, set up in competition with his father was the result of an absurd row that made father and son hate each other. Whatever the ultimate source of their mutual hatred – perhaps the younger George had never forgiven his father for banishing his mother – the presence of the Prince of Wales's rival court forced George I to relinquish the life of quiet retirement that best suited him in order to attempt the creation of a glittering court that would overshadow that of the son he despised. And George did it at Kensington Palace.

Accusations of madness seem to have arrived with the Hanoverians, and not just because George III really was mentally ill. Apart from murdering his wife's lover, George I's hatred of his son – which as we will see was an extraordinarily outlandish hatred – today seems pathological.

George I was mocked by the British for having an extremely fat mistress and an extremely thin one. Schulenburg, the thin one, was known as the giraffe or the maypole and the fat one, Charlotte Kielmansegg, was known as the elephant. They were also known as the elephant and castle largely, it seems, because, recalling a famous area of London, the phrase tripped off the tongue and, besides, kings tended to live in castles. But there were almost certainly bawdy implications – Schulenburg (the castle) had three children by George, and one can imagine Londoners enjoying the ribald overtones when they referred to the king being 'in his castle'.

Charlotte Kielmansegg, the elephant, was in fact George's half-sister and the wife of his Master of the Horse and it seems unlikely that his relationship with her was sexual, although contemporaries certainly thought they were intimately involved. Why, George's enemies asked, does he keep this woman so close to him if she is not his mistress? She was actually the most intelligent member of his family and she took on – along with Melusine von der Schulenburg – the role that might otherwise have been taken by the king's wife, the imprisoned Sophia.

As substitute queens, as it were, Melusine and Charlotte were better housed at Kensington than, for example, George II's mistress Henrietta Howard (who was given those mushroom-infested basement rooms mentioned earlier). In fact, both Melusine and Charlotte were given rooms very close to the king's, although it was not considered appropriate to give either woman the late Queen Anne's apartments, which were left to gather dust. Even a king occasionally had to obey the rules of decorum.

Under George I, power slipped unobtrusively into the hands of Britain's first Prime Minister, Robert Walpole (1676–1745). George was conscious that he had no real power and, knowing that the British public disliked him, he kept a very low profile indeed, hardly even bothering to meet with his ministers unless they insisted. Instead he spent his time at Hampton Court, where he hunted, and at Kensington with his family.

As we have seen, Kensington Palace had been enlarged and enhanced under George's predecessors, but he had his own ideas for improvements that were designed to make visitors to Kensington feel George was a man of taste, a man who could create a palace that would make his visitors gasp. It was almost as if, knowing he lacked political power, the king decided that he would make up the deficit by ensuring he at least had all the trappings of kingship.

He wanted the rooms at Kensington to work in an almost theatrical way so that from the entrance to the palace to the large public rooms where the king would hold court, there would be a succession of ever-grander rooms. He added a magnificent staircase that led into a series of magnificent spaces – the Presence Chamber, the Privy Chamber, the Cupola Room and, finally, the Great Drawing Room. The creation of this new core involved the destruction of the existing central portion of the house – and that central portion was the structure that had been originally built by Sir George Coppin.

The creation of these imposing rooms – which remain largely un-altered today – confirmed George's determination to keep the court at Kensington, but he had additional motives; they were also built to spite his son, George, Prince of Wales (1683–1760). If his son had not set up an alternative court at Leicester Square, the king might well have used Kensington as far more of a private retreat. Instead, as historian Lucy Worsley points out, by 1718 Kensington shone night after night in the glow of garden lanterns as guests strolled about, danced and ate. There were at least fifty or sixty guests most nights and the king walked among the revellers or played cards, bestowing a word here, a comment there.

He probably hated every minute of it but knew that a couple of miles to the east his far more sociable son and daughter-in-law were offering equally extravagant entertainment. He was determined to beat them at their own game and Kensington, being close to London, was far more useful in this battle of the generations than distant Windsor or Hampton Court.

Working hard to make Kensington Palace more attractive, more opulent and therefore more of a draw was only part of the story. In addition to throwing parties and installing sparkling new fittings in the grand reception rooms, George turned his attention to the gardens. Thousands of trees were planted by his gardeners, Charles Bridgeman and Ruth Carpenter – Ruth was the widow of Joseph Carpenter, who, with Bridgeman, had originally been employed to implement the new garden design. It is remarkable that a woman was given such an important job and bears testimony to her knowledge and skill.

The old formal gardens so loved by William and Mary and then Anne were now deeply out of fashion. New gardens emphasised views and at Kensington the prime vistas were out over the Round Pond (created by George II in 1730) and towards what is now the Serpentine, though in the early eighteenth century the latter was still a series of muddy pools along the river Westbourne. But if the landscape had changed, the gardens were still home to the royal collection of animals – including deer, a llama and even, for a while, a tiger.

George I's 'improvements' were nothing compared to those of his daughter-in-law Caroline, who was no doubt delighted to find, upon the death of George I in 1727, that she would now have a free hand at Kensington.

Under her direction, gravelled walks were removed to create large areas of grass – then a sign of wealth and status because keeping a large flat area of closely cropped grass required a huge number of gardeners working with very sharp scythes, something few could afford. Caroline also moved trees and planted new ones, and enlarged the Great Basin, as the Round Pond was then known. It went from being a relatively small oblong to its current large oblong with carefully stepped and rounded corners – it is a shape that ironically can only really be appreciated from the air as the pond covers around seven acres and from a low, pond-side vantage point it is impossible to discern its exact shape.

By 1730, when the Great Basin was enlarged, the animals had vanished – mostly removed to the Royal Menagerie at the Tower of London. Meandering naturalistic paths were created through the woods, and the Westbourne's ponds were finally enlarged to their present appearance as one great lake, then known as the Serpentine River (although as visitors will notice, today there is not much that is serpentine about its shape at all).

Caroline became almost obsessed with her gardening projects at Kensington. She visited other gardens for inspiration – Cliveden and Chiswick House, among others – and her husband, George II, eventually began to complain that her work at Kensington would bankrupt them all.

Caroline was a devoted follower of the landscape gardening fashion promoted by William Kent and Capability Brown. The idea was to create a sense of uninterrupted space and distance and at Kensington this meant views from the East Front of the palace across to the Great Basin and beyond through misty distances to the Serpentine.

Today, the whole landscape gardening revolution of the early eighteenth century can seem to have been to some extent self-contradictory – natural landscapes that did not conform to the new fashion had to be changed artificially to make them look, well, more natural. By the 1730s nothing remained of the formal gardens that William, Mary and Anne had so loved. Only a small brick and stone building – now known as Queen Anne's Alcove – survived these changes. It had formerly been situated in Anne's south garden (on the Kensington High Street side of the palace) so that the queen could sit and view her flowers and plants or escape from the rain. Caroline had it moved to its present position at the Bayswater Road end of the Serpentine.

꙳

In the modern world, George I would be considered the head of an extremely dysfunctional family. Even in his day he was despised and ridiculed – partly because, as we have seen, he went back to Germany as often as he could, but also because of his absurd relationship with his son, which most likely had its origins in the fact that the younger George had not seen his mother since she was imprisoned when he was just eleven. He was never allowed even to refer to his mother's existence, and something of the inner turmoil he must have felt as a result can be judged by the fact that when he inherited the crown and could do as he pleased, he had a portrait of his mother hung in his private apartments. He still never spoke of her, but he would have passed that picture virtually every day for the rest of his life.

On the other hand, George I may well have disliked his son because he reminded him of his imprisoned wife – the wife who had tried to humiliate him by eloping with her lover. Whatever the reason, George I behaved very oddly throughout his life and often in ways that seemed deliberately directed at his son. In *Oddballs and Eccentrics*, Karl Shaw notes that when George I was introduced to his future daughter-in-law, Princess Caroline of Ansbach, he nodded, bowed and then lifted her skirts and looked underneath. Hardly calculated to endear himself to his son and his son's new bride.

Friction was also caused by the fact that George II, the Prince of Wales, was not an entirely submissive son. By the time the prince had reached adulthood and was running his own household, the knowledge that he would one day be king certainly made him resist the demands of his father – demands that extended to absolute compliance in everything. The younger George found this expectation of subservience intolerable.

Things came to a head in what was already a fairly frosty relationship with the christening of the Prince of Wales's son. The king insisted he would choose the godfathers; the Prince of Wales was adamant he would choose. Eventually the son gave way, but at the christening ceremony itself he appeared to challenge the Duke of Newcastle, one of the godfathers chosen by the king, to a duel. The younger George apparently marched up to the duke, shook his fist in his face and said, 'I will fight you!'

In fact, the whole altercation was farcical – George's English pronunciation was so poor that the duke misheard him. He'd actually said, 'I shall find you out!' Or at least that is what the young prince claimed he'd said. The king was not convinced and, besides, bellowing, 'I will find you!', though less threatening than 'I will fight you!', can hardly have been considered friendly.

The king never fully forgave his son, although there was a lukewarm reconciliation in 1720. He had the prince and his wife Caroline evicted from St James's Palace (and Kensington) and wrote to all his relatives telling them that if they visited England and saw his son, they would not be admitted to see the king. Ministers and members of the court were similarly warned.

But because the younger George would inherit on his father's death come what may, many aristocrats and members of the political opposition chose the son over the father – they wagered that if they were loyal to the son, their reward would come when his father died and the prince became king.

For many it was worth the wait, and in the eighteenth century no one imagined that a monarch would rule for the kind of lengthy periods we have come to take for granted with the extraordinarily long reign of Elizabeth II.

❦

A glittering alternative court grew up around the Prince and Princess of Wales at their mansion in Leicester Square. Those who had fallen out with the king and who hoped for future preferment from the next monarch made sure they attended regularly. It is easy to imagine, too, that they would have told the prince he was surely in the right when it came to his dispute with his father.

Just a few miles away at Kensington Palace, those who chose to remain loyal to the king would no doubt have insisted that the son was an ungrateful beast and the king the model of all fathers. In fact, father and son were equally unpleasant.

Part of the problem was that the younger George had in many ways never grown up. Used to getting his way with everyone except his father, he was prone to the most extraordinarily explosive tantrums – he frequently tore off his wig and kicked it around the room in his rage, for example.

Perhaps a key difficulty for both father and son was that they knew the only realm in which they could exercise direct influence was in their relationships with their wives, mistresses, children and courtiers. Real political power, as we have seen, had been subtly taken away from the monarchy, so personal power took on a far greater importance.

This may explain why after George I fell out with his son, he took the prince's three daughters, and the infant son at the centre of the row, and forbade his son and daughter-in-law either to see them or to look after them. The boy (Caroline and George's second son) died soon after being taken to Kensington by the king, and for the rest of their childhoods the prince's daughters were only occasionally allowed to see their parents. Princess Caroline was eventually allowed to see her daughters once a week, but the initial heartless act ended all chance of a rapprochement between father and son.

The girls were looked after by dozens of servants who either lived in the palace or in nearby lodgings, and they lived in material and intellectual luxury; they were, among other accomplishments, taught to play the harpsichord by Handel, a frequent visitor to Kensington Palace.

Of course, they had no need of so many servants, but, like their grand apartments, the massed army of staff reflected the girls' status – even as teenagers they were surrounded by their own courts. Apart from their servants and occasional visitors perhaps hoping to befriend the princesses in order to gain influence with George I, the girls' lives were tightly circumscribed. For their grandfather, Kensington was a fortress where he felt he could be sure his granddaughters would be safe from the influence of their parents. And this was especially so when he set off to spend a summer in Hanover.

One might imagine that having been separated from her children, Caroline, on becoming queen in 1727, would have taken great care not to fall out with them. Yet she grew to hate her eldest son Frederick to such an extent that she frequently spoke of her desire that he should die. This extraordinary attitude must have been linked to the fact that Frederick was raised in Hanover and did not see his parents from when he was seven until he moved to England in 1728 aged twenty-one. But whatever the reason, Frederick was so disliked that George II even planned to ask Parliament if the crown might skip a generation – a fact that Frederick discovered. George also looked at the possibility of splitting his domains so that his favourite son, William, Frederick's younger brother, might inherit Hanover while Frederick took Britain.

In fact, Frederick was to predecease his father George II and it was Caroline's grandson who became George III. In his turn, George III adopted such a puritanical and punishing attitude to his children that *his* son the Prince of Wales, later George IV, rebelled and became one of the most dissolute monarchs in British history, with a string of mistresses and a complete inability to do anything other than eat, drink and pursue other men's wives.

But then George IV's father had been genuinely mad – or at least 'mad' as it was defined in the eighteenth century.

For much of the twentieth century, researchers had agreed that George III's madness was not actually insanity in the strict sense at all. His odd behaviour was caused, so modern medicine seemed to have decided, by porphyria, a disease of the nervous system. However, in more recent years, the weight of opinion has shifted and it is now felt that George III was either periodically psychotic or permanently bipolar. In later life, matters were probably further complicated by what we would now recognise as dementia.

But perhaps this was only an extreme manifestation of a psychological imbalance that afflicted all the Georges – certainly, their inability to get on with their children seems to indicate this. Even the last of the Hanoverians, George IV, though not officially mad, was certainly unbalanced. When still Prince Regent, grossly obese but obsessed with military history, he would regularly talk to his ministers and at dinner with the nobility about his own part in the 1815 Battle of Waterloo. He spoke to everyone as if he had been one of the main commanders at the battle and of course no one dared to contradict him to his face – even though he had actually been at home in England at the time of the battle.

As Adrian Tinniswood recounts in *Behind the Throne*, the Regent's fantasy world eventually produced a particularly bizarre twist when he happened to be seated next to the Duke of Wellington, the hero of Waterloo, at dinner.

The Prince Regent reminded Wellington that during the battle, he, the prince, had been forced to lead his men down a particularly steep slope.

'Yes, very steep, sir,' replied the astonished duke.

The writer Winthrop Mackworth Praed summed up what many thought of the Prince Regent:

> A noble nasty course he ran
> Superbly filthy and fastidious
> He was the world's first gentleman
> And made that appellation hideous.

The wife he hated, Princess Caroline of Brunswick, was equally unpleasant by all accounts but also amusingly unconventional. When asked why she was wearing half a pumpkin on her head (according to Karl Shaw's *Oddballs and Eccentrics*), she replied, 'It is the coolest sort of coiffure.'

According to Shaw, Caroline seems to have made a point of being eccentric – having recently arrived in England, she was asked to meet a group of war veterans. When she saw them lined up to meet her, she said, 'Mein Gott … have all the English only one arm and one leg?' She also allegedly had her portrait painted naked from the waist up.

CHAPTER FIVE

PAINTED HARLOTS

Most gracious queen, we thee implore
To go away and sin no more
But if that effort be too great
To go away at any rate.

<small>ANONYMOUS EPIGRAM ON QUEEN CAROLINE</small>

The eccentric behaviour of George IV and his wife was many years in the future when George I decided that although, following the work initiated by William and Mary, Kensington Palace was now large enough to meet the requirements of the royal family, it was still not suitably decorated. George's obsession with the idea that Kensington must outshine the court created at Leicester Square prompted a decorative scheme that is both unique and uniquely important.

Initially, the decision to decorate the house in a manner befitting a king led to another row, this time between two painters and their supporters.

Everyone expected George to approach the most fashionable painter of the day – the artist Sir James Thornhill (1675 or '76–1734). Thornhill had already painted ceilings at St Paul's Cathedral, the Naval Hospital at Greenwich and at Hampton Court. But success had gone to his head and when it came to the commission to design and paint the interior at Kensington Palace he overreached himself – or more precisely, he overpriced himself – and was rejected. His career never recovered.

Thornhill had offered to carry out the work on the Cupola Room for £800 and although this was expensive by the standards of the day, he was also unlucky in terms of timing. He may have been an established, revered figure but his work was well known and perhaps a little unexciting. As with art across the ages, the new man with new ideas was always likely to have the edge over older, more established artists and that was especially true if he happened to be cheaper. In the 1720s the up-and-coming man was William Kent, who offered to paint the same room at Kensington for only £300.

Today it is difficult to understand how Kent managed to captivate the establishment in quite the way he did. A coach painter from Yorkshire, Kent arrived in London knowing no one and quickly transformed himself into the champion of the new and very fashionable Palladian style. It is true that he had studied in Italy, but it was the friendship he skilfully cultivated with Lord Burlington that really launched his career. To this day, Burlington's house at Chiswick, as designed by Kent, is seen as the finest and earliest example of Palladian architecture and landscape gardening in Britain.

Kent simply couldn't put a foot wrong: by the time he died in 1748 he had worked on Burlington House in Piccadilly, the Treasury building in Whitehall and the buildings overlooking Horse Guards Parade. He also designed furniture and advised on what today would be called interior design. Despite his humble birth, he seems to have been remarkably charismatic, especially when it came to aristocratic patrons. Lord Burlington positively doted on him.

But in the 1720s, George I had another good reason not to offer the redecoration of Kensington to James Thornhill – the older painter had already been commissioned by the king's hated son and daughter-in-law.

Kent was unsullied by such associations and George I offered him the work that was to help make his name, but the decision caused uproar in the art establishment. Thornhill's friends were furious at the promotion of this unknown upstart and they did as much as they could to blacken Kent's name. All attempts to persuade the king to reverse his decision and offer the work to Thornhill failed, but there was a concession. A commission of established artists was established to oversee the work at Kensington and to ensure, ostensibly, that Kent was up to the mark and didn't cheat his royal employer.

In fact, the commission was made up of Thornhill's friends, so it was bound to criticise Kent's work. Sure enough, no sooner had Kent begun work than the commission began to report that he just wasn't up to the job. They even suggested he had cheated the king by charging for an expensive paint while actually using a cheaper substitute. Despite the commission's recommendations, Kent continued to paint at Kensington.

But Kent was not an easy man to get on with. He made enemies easily – he was also greedy, careless of other artists' sensitivities and irritatingly good at courting the rich and influential. William Hogarth loathed Kent – in a famous engraving he shows a stone portico with a statue of an artist standing above it. The artist is clearly intended to be William Kent, but beneath the figure on the portico Hogarth has misspelled his name. Instead of Kent there are three letters: KNT. Anyone looking at the engraving in the early eighteenth century would have known what Hogarth meant by those three letters. Only the most outrageous word in the English language would do for this upstart. How ironic, then, that both Kent and Hogarth are buried not far from each other in the same small churchyard at Chiswick.

Whatever his enemies said about him, Kent was unassailable. By 1718, according to Ernest Law, writing in 1908, Kent had even eased the great Christopher Wren out of his job at Kensington.

Kent's work at the palace took several years to complete, but it is a myth to say that it has always been universally admired. To some extent, we are so delighted to find anything in London from the seventeenth and eighteenth centuries that has not been demolished, remodelled or painted over that we are likely to be overly enthusiastic about almost anything that survives.

The writer Ernest Law, whose history of Kensington Palace was published in 1906, thought Kent's changes to Wren's state rooms were deplorable and even the famous decorative work on the king's staircase at Kensington failed to meet with his approval. He liked the Cupola Room – a room consistently praised for its extraordinary gilded ceiling, giving the impression of a lofty dome, which it is not. But Law hated the picture of Jupiter and Semele on the ceiling of the King's

Drawing Room. He thought Semele reclining on a couch 'ridiculous'. 'No painting could be worse,' he said.

But then Law seems to have been a curmudgeonly critic – he also deplored Kent's destruction of the formal gardens created by Queen Anne. Fashions had changed once again by the late nineteenth and early twentieth centuries and Law thought landscape gardening 'destructive and desolating'.

The most remarkable part of Kent's decorative scheme at Kensington is undoubtedly the King's Staircase, painted in the 1720s. Again, Law thought it poor-quality work and he was not alone. Horace Walpole wrote that Kent's painting at Kensington and elsewhere was 'below mediocrity', though he admired his landscape gardening. Kent was certainly no Rubens, but perhaps the slightly rough edge to his work on the staircase at Kensington is one of the reasons we admire it today – it is somehow in keeping with the figures that stare out at us: servants, courtiers and odd eccentrics who had found a place either above or below stairs at court.

For us it is the presence of these often ordinary characters – the sort of people who were very rarely painted before the twentieth century – that outweighs any sense that the painting technique is not of the finest. For Ernest Law, painting servants rather than grandees may have detracted from the appeal of the staircase. Certainly, the staircase had fallen badly into disrepair – Law describes 'the woeful state of dust, filth, decay and rot', and if that is any reflection on the state of the rest of the palace, it is not surprising that there were moves around this time to have the whole palace pulled down. It was only deference to Queen Victoria's wishes that saved it.

Whatever one thinks of the paintings on the staircase, they are remarkable in that they depict a large number of the ordinary people who lived and worked at the palace at the time.

Portraying servants in this way is not quite unique – it was famously done at Erddig, the home of the eccentric Yorke family in north Wales, where servants were painted again and again through many generations.

There are forty-five portraits of palace inhabitants on the staircase at Kensington Palace. Some can no longer be identified, but they almost certainly include, according to Ernest Law, 'a young man in Polish dress representing a certain Mr Ulric, a page of the King's admired by the court … for the elegance and beauty of his person'; a page of Lady Suffolk's who (again according to Ernest Law) was a Quaker; and two Muslims, Mohammed and Mustapha, who were George I's favourite servants. Intriguingly, there is also a portrait of a man holding a key, which suggests that he was probably the housekeeper at Kensington. If so, this would have been Henry Lowman, housekeeper for a remarkable twenty-seven years (1700–27). Who knows, among the other unidentified servants there may be the letter writer to foreign potentates, the mole catcher, the 'necessary woman' and the yeoman of the salt cellar. Perhaps best of all there is a portrait of a rather fat, jolly-looking man wearing a turban – this is the painter William Kent himself. Behind Kent there is a portrait of his mistress, Elizabeth Butler.

There is also a portrait of a boy about whom little is known except that he was kept as a sort of pet by George I, having been found living wild, naked and unable to speak in a forest in Germany (or so the story goes). The life of the so-called Wild Boy is neatly summed up by William Henry Pyne in his *History of Royal Residences* published in 1819:

He was sent over to England in April 1726 and ... brought before his majesty and the nobility. He could not speak and scarce had any idea of things but was pleased with the ticking of a watch, the splendid dresses of the king and princess and endeavoured to put on his own hand a glove that was given to him by her royal highness.

He was dressed in gaudy habiliments but at first disliked this confinement and much difficulty was found in making him lie on a bed; he however, soon walked upright and often sat for his picture. He was at first entrusted to the care of the philosophical Dr Arbuthnot who had him baptised Peter; but notwithstanding all the doctor's pains, he was unable to bring him to the use of speech or to the pronunciation of words ... He resisted all instruction and existed as a person allowed in succession by the three sovereigns in whose reigns he lived. He resided latterly at a farm near Berkhampsted in Hertfordshire until February 1785 where he died at the supposed age of nearly ninety.

Peter and his carer Dr Arbuthnot are among the most intriguing of all the portraits on the staircase – Peter smiling touchingly and Dr Arbuthnot standing a little behind him but full of solicitude for his charge. Peter carries a few oak leaves in his hand – a hint, to those who know, of his origins in that German forest.

Other portraits include a beautiful woman in a black hood – she is probably Princess Caroline's milliner – and most intriguingly of all there are those remarkable portraits of George I's favourite 'servants of the body', Mustapha and Mohammed. Intelligent and kindly, they stare out with the reassuring gaze one can imagine George liked so well.

So far as we know, the two Muslim servants were originally prisoners of war. According to Ernest Law, their history was pretty straightforward:

> [They] were taken prisoner by the Imperialists in Hungary. At the raising of the Siege of Vienna in 1685, George I … was wounded and was attended by these two Turks …who were said to have saved his life … King George on his accession to the British throne brought these two faithful servants with him.

Amusingly, Mohammed and Mustapha were the only servants to whom George would confess he suffered from haemorrhoids, or piles, but then this was probably unavoidable since the two men helped him with almost every intimate activity, dressing and washing him and accompanying him to the lavatory.

Both men became wealthy during their long years with George and in fact Mohammed attended the king until his own death in 1726; Mustapha did so until the king's death the following year. Mohammed was given the title Keeper of the King's Closet; as a result, he was courted by the great and good, who knew that without Mohammed's agreement they would not gain admittance to the king's more intimate gatherings. At the end of his life, Mohammed did something quite remarkable. Ernest Law takes up the story: '[Mohammed] in whatever way he may have obtained his wealth, made a noble and benevolent use of it; for, among many other recorded acts of benevolence, he released from prison about three hundred poor debtors by paying their harsh creditors.'

Perhaps what we love most today about the portraits on the staircase is that they give us a glimpse into the lives of people whose deeds (and even existences) were only very rarely recorded in earlier centuries, for servants in the early eighteenth century really were considered lesser beings in a way that is hard for us to comprehend today.

The Hanoverian kings may have been mad, bad or both, but the now discredited idea that noble birth and aristocratic or regal blood counted for everything held the minds of our Georgian ancestors in an unquestioned and unquestioning way. William may have been a dullard; George I may have been dull, vindictive and even murderous, but in their veins flowed royal blood and in the early eighteenth century that mattered above all else.

Having redecorated his palace at Kensington, George I settled into a curious routine that lasted for the rest of his life. He reluctantly made himself available to his ministers and the nobility each day, though as he grew older even this became less frequent. He sat with his mistress Melusine and his three illegitimate daughters every evening for precisely three hours. He allowed his three granddaughters to pray (several times a day), walk in the gardens, play shuttlecock and eat. They were prisoners, but in a gilded cage – they attended balls and parties, danced, sang and played, and each week they were given a new pair of shoes.

But despite insisting that the court remain at Kensington and despite all his work to beautify the palace, George was still much happier in Germany and few doubt that if he could have had his way he would have remained there. As we have seen, he spent numerous summers there, and was clearly reluctant to return. When he was at Kensington, such was his desire for a private life that he would use the servants' staircases and corridors, of which there are still a number at Kensington, to avoid being pestered by his own courtiers.

For the first three years of George I's reign he was based at St James's Palace, not because he preferred it to Kensington but because Kensington was being made ready for him. He travelled down the Kensington road regularly, however, to keep an eye on the artists and craftsmen at work. Once the palace was ready he stayed permanently at Kensington (except when he was in Hanover, or hunting at Hampton Court) and travelled up to St James's when necessary to meet his ministers, especially the German ones he himself had appointed – they were the only politicians he could understand, for he spoke very little English.

The architects and designers who worked at Kensington in this period included William Benson, an amateur architect much favoured by George, not because he was a particularly good architect but because he was a Whig. The king heartily disliked the Tories, suspecting them of being secret Jacobite sympathisers. The Scottish architect Colen Campbell was at Kensington for a time, as was Sir Thomas Hewett, an enthusiast for the latest Italianate fashions. Hewett helped create the interiors of the Cupola Room, Drawing Room and Privy Chamber at Kensington – all survive more or less as they were finished by Campbell and Hewett.

Astonishingly, even without the Prince and Princess of Wales and their numerous servants – they were not allowed even to approach the palace – George I's court still amounted to more than one thousand people. This included dozens of German servants. It was a tremendous squeeze to fit them all into the palace even after it had been greatly increased in size, which is why the maids of honour had to live in Kensington Square and why numerous other courtiers (and would-be courtiers) lodged here and there all over the village of Kensington.

George didn't have long to enjoy Kensington Palace or his British dominions. As historian Adrian Tinniswood neatly puts it, he enjoyed best those days when he was either setting off for Hanover or going from his bedroom to his lavatory to his garden to his mistress and then back to bed. And it was during his journey home to Germany in 1727 that he died. He became ill and died at Osnabruck, almost certainly from a stroke. The last British monarch to die overseas, he was buried at Herrenhausen in the family mausoleum.

Back in England, the Prince of Wales – now, of course, George II – no doubt rejoiced at the news of his father's death. At the very least the new king could no longer be kept away from his daughters. An ascension with positive personal repercussions for George was seen as anything but positive in the public sphere. George might have thought he would be popular with his people, following his Anglophobic father, but it was not to be. He was unpopular from the start, though not quite as unpopular as his father had been – perhaps in part because his

English was much better than his father's, but also because he decided to dispense with the services of many of his German advisers.

George I had retained them throughout his reign largely because he felt more comfortable with his fellow countrymen.

Having been hated by his father George I, one might have thought George II would be careful not to fall out with *his* son. But it was not to be. George II was destined to hate his own son and heir, Frederick, just as much as he had himself been hated by his father.

Part of the problem was simply that George had left Frederick in Hanover, where he had been born in 1707. Father and son saw nothing of each other until 1728 and when they did, the father decided almost immediately that he heartily disliked the son, a situation that remained unchanged until the end of Frederick's life in 1751. On hearing the news of Frederick's premature death, George II was delighted – it meant his grandson, whom he much preferred, could ascend the throne as George III.

From the day of his arrival in England, Frederick seemed to get nothing right. And in an extraordinary example of history repeating itself, it was a row over a new-born child that was to lead to the final rift between father and son. In the meantime, there were endless petty squabbles.

Whenever George and Frederick were at Kensington together, something would go wrong. They seemed eternally destined to irritate each other. For weeks Frederick and his wife Augusta infuriated Queen Caroline by, for example, deliberately arriving late at the chapel at Kensington. To get to their seats Frederick and Augusta had to squeeze past Caroline, which meant she had to get up to let them pass. This continued until Caroline could stand it no longer. She told her son and his wife that they must use an alternative entrance. Frederick immediately took this as the most dreadful slight and refused ever to attend chapel again. The situation is further complicated by the fact that, as some historians, including Barbara Clay Finch in her book *Lives of the Princesses of Wales*, have pointed out, it was Frederick who consistently forced Augusta to be late. So when Caroline ordered them to use another entrance, it provided Frederick with a pretext to forbid Augusta from attending chapel at all.

Terrified that Frederick would set up an alternative court as he himself had done, George felt he had to allow Frederick to attend the court at Kensington – although it was a standing joke that they ignored each other completely despite being in the same room.

But when Augusta became pregnant in 1736, Frederick did something for which the king never forgave him. In the final stages of her pregnancy, Augusta and Frederick were staying at Hampton Court when the couple realised that Augusta was going into labour. Without permission from the king, Frederick dragged his wife out of bed, called for a carriage and drove through the night so the baby would be born at St James's, away from his hated parents, who would have insisted on being present at the birth.

When the king and queen woke, they raced across London to catch up with their son and daughter-in-law.

They were furious that Frederick had acted without permission, but they were more concerned – almost obsessively so – that Frederick and Augusta had run off to give themselves time to find a healthy male baby to switch with their own new-born. Caroline may even have thought the pregnancy was a pretence or that Augusta had been made pregnant by someone other than her son. Her suspicions were legion and verging on the paranoid. Some time earlier she had insisted in public that she thought her own son incapable of fathering a child and it was this that lay behind her suspicions. Her hatred of him seems to have known no bounds. According to Lord Hervey's memoirs, once, upon catching sight of Frederick through a window, the queen said, 'Look, there he goes. That wretch! That villain! I wish the ground would open this moment and sink the monster to the lowest hole in hell!'

Nonetheless, when she arrived at St James's and discovered Augusta had given birth to a girl, Caroline calmed down – this couldn't be a 'bed-pan heir' since it was just a girl and, as she quickly pointed out, not a very sturdy one at that.

But the act of disobedience in leaving Hampton Court without permission was too much for the king. He immediately wrote to his family and to his ministers and other members of the court to say that if anyone had anything to do with his son and daughter-in-law they would not be allowed into the presence of the king ever again. It was an exact re-run of the rift between George II and his father George I. Frederick and Augusta were unceremoniously forced to leave Kensington Palace and Frederick's evenings playing the cello at the palace came to an abrupt end.

What Caroline and George hated more than anything was that, constitutionally, they could not stop Frederick becoming king – although fate was to take a hand and Frederick never did become king, dying in 1751. His mother Caroline died in 1737, long before her grandson George III was crowned upon the death of her husband the king in 1760.

The rift between father and son actually worked to Frederick's advantage in many ways – he knew this, of course, and encouraged those who chose him over his father to believe that when he became king they would receive their reward. For the courtiers and hangers-on at Kensington and Hampton Court it was a choice – rewards and favours now, or rewards and favours later. For those who had not been able to ingratiate themselves with the father, or who had fallen out with him, the son offered new and perhaps more lucrative possibilities provided they were prepared to wait.

Like his father, George II kept the court at Kensington and like his father he also returned to Hanover each summer as often as he could. But this created a problem: while he was away, often for months at a time, who was to rule? The answer should have been that 'monster' – his hated son – and his despised daughter-in-law, Augusta.

But George was having none of it. Instead, he left his wife Caroline as Regent, a position to which – as was almost universally agreed at the time – she was ideally suited. In fact, she would have made a far better monarch than her dull-witted husband. She took the business of government very seriously, enjoyed political discussions and no doubt revelled in her chance to show how astute she was.

Whenever George was away, she insisted on regular meetings with her Privy Council and held public days at Kensington on Sundays when anyone who looked and sounded right might be admitted – hundreds usually turned up and jostled for places in the state rooms. Interesting or important foreign visitors were also welcomed to Kensington – the great Italian castrato Farinelli visited in 1734 and the court was astonished (according to some reports; others insist it was planned) when a group from the Yamacraw Native American tribe from Georgia reached Kensington – what especially shocked the court was the fact that they wore no trousers and had painted faces – requesting an audience with the king. They had come as a deputation asking the monarch for protection against the depredations of the European settlers in America. Needless to say, no protection was ever offered or forthcoming.

Courtiers at Kensington were impressed – often grudgingly so – at how Caroline dealt with these and other visitors. George seemed ill at ease; Caroline, by contrast, was very much in command.

A contemporaneous satirical verse captured the truth of Caroline's superior qualities perfectly:

> You may strut, dapper George, but 'twill all be in vain,
> We all know 'tis Queen Caroline not you, that reign –
> You govern no more than Don Philip of Spain
> Then if you would have us fall down and adore you
> Lock up your fat spouse as your dad did before you.

George was in Hanover for lengthy periods during 1729, 1732, 1735 and 1736 and at these times Caroline not only hosted visitors but also dealt with the regular business of meeting ministers and discussing the issues of the day – her grasp of politics was said to far exceed that of her husband, whose only interests were hunting deer at Hampton Court and telling endless anecdotes about his days as a soldier.

Despite her almost deranged hatred of her first-born son, Caroline doted on her third son, as did her husband. This third son, perceived by his family as beyond reproach, was the infamous Duke of Cumberland, who almost succeeded single-handedly in turning the British from Catholic haters to Catholic sympathisers. The reason was that, having defeated the Jacobites decisively at Culloden in 1746, 'Butcher Cumberland' (as he became known to his Tory enemies) pursued the survivors and their families across the Highlands, destroying everything in his path. Whole families and even their livestock were wiped out. For the rest of his life, Cumberland was criticised in certain quarters, especially among Tories, for his actions following Culloden, and he was baffled. He was convinced that he had done his country a great service and that far from being censured he should have been richly rewarded. The fact that this didn't happen made him resentful and bitter. His actions at Culloden may have had one other effect – they almost certainly contributed to his father's increasing unpopularity, although George's reputation as the 'absent king' (thanks to all those summers in Hanover) may well have had far more to do with it. Certainly, there was a general feeling that Caroline should not have been so frequently left holding the reins.

CHAPTER SIX

GILDED WINGS

'There are three sexes: men, women and Herveys.'
LADY MARY WORTLEY MONTAGU

'Show me some good person about that court; find me, among those selfish courtiers, those dissolute gay people, someone I can love and regard.'
ROBERT WALPOLE

Caroline made Kensington the centre of a new sort of cultural life in England. Unlike her Hanoverian predecessors, she delighted in the company of philosophers and intellectuals. Voltaire wrote of her, 'I must say that despite all her titles and crowns, this princess was born to encourage the arts and the well-being of mankind; even on the throne she is a benevolent philosopher; and she has never lost an opportunity to learn or to manifest her generosity.'

As a young woman, before she came to England she had corresponded regularly with the German philosopher Gottfried Leibniz (1646–1716). In England she had more time to devote to intellectual matters, as we know from the diaries of Lord Hervey (1696–1743), a courtier who became Caroline's great confidant and friend, and a figure who dominated court life at Kensington for many years.

The fact of Caroline's friendship with Hervey is all the more astonishing because earlier in life Hervey had been the close companion (and almost certainly lover) of Caroline's hated son Frederick. The two fell out as adults but had been very close in their early years. Hervey's contemporaries were convinced that he was homosexual, despite the fact that he was married with children.

The great Augustan poet Alexander Pope gets close to openly declaring Hervey's homosexuality when he portrays him as Sporus in the *Epistle to Dr Arbuthnot*:

> Let Sporus tremble—'What? That thing of silk,
> Sporus, that mere white curd of ass's milk?
> Satire or sense, alas! Can Sporus feel?
> Who breaks a butterfly upon a wheel?'
> Yet let me flap this bug with gilded wings,
> This painted child of dirt that stinks and stings;
> Whose buzz the witty and the fair annoys,
> Yet wit ne'er tastes, and beauty ne'r enjoys,
> So well-bred spaniels civilly delight
> In mumbling of the game they dare not bite.
> Eternal smiles his emptiness betray,
> As shallow streams run dimpling all the way.
> Whether in florid impotence he speaks,
> And, as the prompter breathes, the puppet squeaks;
> Or at the ear of Eve, familiar toad,

Half froth, half venom, spits himself abroad,

In puns, or politics, or tales, or lies,

Or spite, or smut, or rhymes, or blasphemies.

His wit all see-saw, between that and this,

Now high, now low, now Master up, now Miss,

And he himself one vile antithesis.

Amphibious thing! That acting either part,

The trifling head, or the corrupted heart,

Fop at the toilet, flatt'rer at the board,

Now trips a lady, and now struts a lord.

Hervey was almost certainly bisexual, and the great love of his life was Stephen Fox – or Stu, as Hervey addressed his friend in his letters – with whom he lived on and off for ten years. When Hervey's descendants were preparing to publish his diaries in the nineteenth century, they destroyed the section dealing with his relationship with Fox. One can merely assume they were appalled, as only the Victorians could be, at what they read. Due to his hatred of Hervey, Pope cannot be seen as an objective judge of his character, but Hervey's ambiguous nature was something generally acknowledged. His feminine traits may also explain, at least in part, his friendship with Queen Caroline, who clearly adopted an almost sisterly interest in him. Certainly, contemporaries found Hervey rather effeminate. Romney Sedgwick, who edited the 1952 edition of Hervey's memoirs, reminds us that even Hervey's friend Lady Mary Wortley Montagu commented, 'There are three sexes: men, women and Herveys.'

Many young, witty men who tried their luck at Kensington during George II's reign were not so lucky as Hervey, whose charm and humour were legendary. John Gay, famous for his play *The Beggar's Opera*, visited Kensington on numerous occasions in the hope not just of preferment but also of patronage. Unlike many who attended court and failed to win the attentions of a member of the royal family, Gay was able to vent his anger – after he'd given up – in verse. Gay was taken up by a number of aristocrats outside court circles, including the Duchess of Queensbury, who was actually dismissed from court for trying to get people to subscribe to his ballad opera *Polly*.

Gay was talented but dangerous – *The Beggar's Opera* was seen as a satire on the ruling classes, who could rob, cheat and lie without punishment while the poor were punished harshly for the slightest misdemeanour.

Gay goes out of his way in his *Fables* to criticise the court, which is odd given that the *Fables* were written for George and Caroline's second son:

> One time I lived in town like you.
> I was a courtier born and bred,
> And kings have bent to me the head.
> I knew each lord and lady's passion,
> And fostered every vice in fashion.
> But Jove was wrath—loves not the liar—
> He sent me here to cool my fire,
> Retained my nature—but he shaped
> My form to suit the thing I aped,
> And sent me in this shape obscene,
> To batten in a sylvan scene.
> How different is your lot and mine!

> Lo! how you eat, and drink, and dine;
> Whilst I, condemned to thinnest fare,
> Like those I flattered, feed on air.

Pope, though much admired, was considered a dangerous character and he too failed at court – everyone knew he might smile and talk brilliantly but then go home and write a most terrible lampoon. He was also a Catholic, and though a great wit, was small and hunchbacked. But the fact that he did not do well at Kensington led him to attack the institution he saw as rejecting him:

> To one fair lady out of Court,
> And two fair ladies in,
> Who think the Turk and Pope a sport,
> And wit and love no sin!
> Come, these soft lines, with nothing stiff in,
> To Bellenden, Lepell, and Griffin.
> With a fa, la, la.
> Alas! like Schutz I cannot pun,
> Like Grafton court the Germans;
> Tell Pickenbourg how slim she's grown,
> Like Meadows run to sermons;
> To court ambitious men may roam,
> But I and Marlbro' stay at home.

Pope here names the famous Molly Lepell, who married Lord Hervey in 1720, as one of the great beauties of the Kensington court. Pope could never have been accused of being tactful – as well as making his admiration for people he favoured clear, he took great risks and attacked anyone he felt had slighted him. He did not have the subtle courtier's diplomatic gifts. Lord Hervey inspired Pope's dislike precisely because he was the consummate courtier who spent years at Kensington as Queen Caroline's closest confidant.

Hervey made up for the fact that George continually humiliated Caroline, confiding acidly to his diaries, 'Everybody shared the warm and frequent sallies of his abominable temper.'

Again and again Hervey reiterates how irritable and vindictive George could be: 'She could never speak one word uncontradicted,' he tells us. Occasionally his accounts of life at Kensington are especially vivid, as here when he describes an evening's entertainment:

His Majesty stayed about five minutes in the gallery, snubbed the Queen, who was drinking chocolate, for always stuffing; the Princess Emily for not hearing him; the Princess Caroline for being grown fat; the Duke of Cumberland for standing awkwardly; Lord Hervey for not knowing what relation the Prince of Sultzbach was to the Elector Palatine, and then carried the Queen to walk and be resnubbed in the garden.

Hervey may not have been an entirely objective observer, but it is difficult to find anyone who attended the court at Kensington who has a good word to say about George, who was so self-important that he couldn't even take a joke and was famous for overreacting when he felt he was not getting the attention he deserved. Hervey describes an incident that occurred during one of George's parties:

One evening Princess Emily pulled away Lady Deloraine's chair as she went to sit at cards. She fell sprawled on the floor. The king roared with laughter. Two days later Lady Deloraine got her revenge by playing the same trick on the king who was furious and banished her from court for some time.

Yet the relationship between George and Caroline, a relationship played out both intimately and publicly at Kensington, was more complex than Hervey suggests. Despite his bad temper and boorishness, there was a tender side to the king – a side that he seems to have been at great pains to hide for much of the time. When Caroline contracted smallpox, for example, George insisted on staying by her side, even though that meant he too was at risk of contracting a disease that was frequently fatal.

And when Caroline died – horribly and in great pain from a perforated gut – George never ceased to mourn her loss. The unkind suggested, with some degree of truth, that this was because she was the only member of the family who never contradicted or criticised him. She made his life easy by giving him the kind of complete obedience denied him by his son; and indeed, by his ministers and the population of Britain in general.

But when Caroline was well and in sparkling form at Kensington it often looked as if George hated her. He was aware that she was considered the more intelligent and inevitably his resentment boiled up – by putting her down in public he felt at some level he was restoring the balance. He was showing his courtiers and other visitors that regardless of her brilliance, he was still the king.

Despite her quick wit and occasional cutting remarks to others, she meekly accepted the king's stinging attacks and this was typical of her attitude throughout her life. Occasionally she made a mistake and did something without consulting him or at least asking for his advice and he would be furious. Hervey recounts the famous case of the changed pictures in the king's rooms at Kensington.

In the absence of the King, the Queen had taken several very bad pictures out of the great drawing room at Kensington and put very good ones in their places. The King, affecting, for the sake of contradiction, to dislike this change or from his extreme ignorance of painting, really disapproving it, told Lord Hervey as vice-chamberlain, that he would have every new picture taken away and every old one replaced. Lord Hervey who had a mind to make his court to the Queen by opposing this order, asked if his Majesty would not give leave for the two Van Dykes, at least on each side of the chimney to remain, instead of those two sign posts done by nobody knew who, that had been removed to make way for them. To which the king answered, 'My lord I have a great respect for your taste in what you understand, but in pictures I beg leave to follow my own. I suppose you assisted the Queen with your fine advice when she was pulling my house to pieces and spoiling all my furniture. Thank God at least she has left the walls standing. As for the Van Dykes I do not care whether they are changed or no, but for the picture with the dirty frame over the door and the three nasty little children, I will have them taken away and the old ones restored; I will have it done too tomorrow morning before I go to London or else I know it will not be done at all.'

'Would your Majesty' said Hervey, 'have the gigantic fat Venus restored too?'

'Yes, my lord, I am not so nice as your lordship. I like my fat Venus much better than anything you have given me instead of her.'

Lord Hervey thought that if his Majesty had liked his fat Venus as well as he used to do, there would have been none of these disputations.

Hervey was so important to the queen during her years at Kensington that no sooner had her husband left the palace for whatever reason than she sent out a messenger to summon Hervey. If she was still in bed, Hervey claims in his memoirs, she would ask him to join her in her bedroom – a serious breach of etiquette, but one that shows just how important Hervey was to her.

Caroline's influence with George was far greater than his disparaging remarks about her might lead us to believe – she knew how to handle him and get what she wanted despite the fact that he was often rude to her. In private he listened carefully to her advice because he knew she had a far better grasp of public affairs. Perhaps what he saw as the humiliation of having to take her advice in this way created a desire to exact revenge on her in public.

The most likely means of gaining access to George I was generally agreed to be through his mistress Melusine. George II's mistresses were far less useful in this regard – Caroline was the route to the king – despite the fact that his primary mistress for more than twenty years was one of the most brilliant women of her generation.

Melusine (who was, as it were, a substitute wife for George I) was given high-status apartments at Kensington, while a generation later Henrietta Howard (1689–1767), as we have seen, was confined to those famously damp basement rooms where mushrooms were said to grow on the walls. However, when Henrietta was finally allowed to leave the court, she retreated to the wonderful Marble Hill House at Twickenham, which George had had built for her when he was Prince of Wales.

Like Caroline, Henrietta had to suffer George II's regular bouts of ill temper, but despite that, she was a woman he found he could not do without. She had accepted George's initial overtures, and agreed to become his mistress, in large part to escape her violent, drunken husband Charles, 9th Earl of Suffolk. It was a shrewd move that made her both rich and loved. Both Alexander Pope and John Gay agreed she was one of the very few people at Kensington who was honest, straightforward, intelligent and loyal. Gay wrote of her:

> O wonderful creature, a woman of reason,
> Never grave out of pride, never gay out of season
> When so easy to guess who this angel should be
> Who would think Mrs Howard ne're dreamt it was she.

Pope, who visited Henrietta at Marble Hill House for many years after her retirement from court, was equally keen to praise her:

> I know a thing that's most uncommon –
> Envy be silent and attend!
> I know a reasonable woman,
> Handsome yet witty and a friend.

By 'reasonable' Pope meant not that she was moderate and sensible (the modern meaning) but that Henrietta was able to think for herself – she was able to reason, a quality considered pre-eminently masculine in the eighteenth century. Henrietta and Pope also shared a hatred of court life – Henrietta spent years trying to obtain permission to retire, but worries about her husband kept her close to the king, probably as much (given her husband's violent tendencies) for reasons of personal safety as anything else. And her worries about her husband proved to be well founded when he turned up at Kensington Palace one night, drunk and in a foul temper. He had climbed over the gates to the park and staggered to the main door of the palace where his clothes and generally aristocratic appearance (even though he was drunk) persuaded the night porter to admit him. He made such a scene before the household – though not, apparently, in front of the king – that he was offered £2,000 to shut up and go away permanently. He took the money and vanished.

But if there were one or two people at Kensington who seemed to rise above the egotistical, grasping mass, most courtiers were pretty awful, although it is a curious fact of court life that most of the complaints about the extended royal community came from the courtiers themselves. They invariably suggested that they were themselves decent, honest men; it was all the other courtiers who were the problem.

Robert Walpole wrote of George II's court: 'Show me some good person about that court; find me, among those selfish courtiers, those dissolute gay people, someone I can love and regard.'

Walpole's view of the court at Kensington – and indeed at Hampton Court, Windsor and St James's, for the same fools and rogues assembled at each of these places when they could – was not particularly biased. It is hard to find a writer who has a good word to say about life at court at this or indeed at any time before the modern era.

John Hervey is quite measured in the following account of a courtier's day; here he is writing about Hampton Court, but he might just as easily be describing the court at Kensington. In a letter to Lady Sundoe he writes:

I will not trouble you with any account of our occupations at Hampton Court. No mill horse ever went in a more constant track or a more unchanging circle; so that, by the assistance of an almanack for the day of the week, and a watch for the hour of the day, you may inform yourself fully, without any other intelligences but your memory, of every transaction within the verge of the court.

Walking, chaises, levees and audiences fill the morning. At night the king plays at commerce and backgammon (and the queen at Quadrille), where poor Lady Charlotte runs her usual nightly gauntlet, the queen pulling her hood and the Princess Royal rapping her knuckles. The Duke of Rutland takes his nightly opiate of lottery, and sleeps as usual between the princesses Amelia and Caroline. Lord Grantham strolls from one room to another … like some discontented ghost that oft appears and is forbid to speak and stirs himself about as people stir a fire not with any design, but in hopes to make it burn brisker.

At last the king gets up, the pool finishes and everybody has their dismission. Their majesties retire to Lady Charlotte and my Lord Lifford; my Lord Grantham to Lady Frances and Mr Clarke; some to supper, some to bed and thus the evening and the morning make the day.

There is something intensely world-weary yet not quite cynical about this account, which has the ring of truth (or something very close to it).

Always playing second fiddle to a man of far less intelligence than herself, Caroline seems ultimately to have sublimated her intellectual enthusiasms – beyond discussions with Hervey and other friends – and replaced them with an intelligent passion for gardening and pictures. She, rather than George, collected artwork from other royal palaces to show at Kensington – she wanted royal portraits to drive home the idea that she and her husband were not German incomers but rather retained a direct bloodline from the Stuarts and earlier monarchs. This was important given that George was unpopular precisely because even those not obviously Jacobite in their sympathies really did still think it was absurd to offer the British crown to a family that had started out governing a tiny principality in Germany.

❦

It is difficult to imagine, now that valuable pictures today are carefully catalogued and kept under lock and key, but in George II's time at Kensington, pictures and drawings – even by the greatest Italian masters – were sometimes stuffed into drawers and cupboards or left stacked against the wall of some ante-room or service corridor.

Ernest Law recounts how Caroline hunted through cupboards bursting with papers only to discover a series of magnificent Holbein drawings that she promptly put up in the state rooms at Kensington. She bought and borrowed pictures of earlier monarchs from some of Britain's oldest families – Lord Cornwallis, for example, provided pictures of various Tudor and Stuart monarchs including James I and Charles I, Henry VIII and his daughter Elizabeth I. Caroline was careful to hang portraits of herself and her husband among these pictures. It was a subtle act of self-promotion that would not have gone unnoticed by courtiers and visitors to the palace from across Europe.

If picture-collecting was to some extent a public relations exercise, the same cannot be said for Caroline's devotion to the gardens at Kensington; that was genuine and personal, and much of what we enjoy in the gardens today is her legacy.

The gardens were initially opened to the public on Saturdays only and they were patrolled, according to Thomas Faulkner in his *History and Antiquities of Kensington*, by 'an increasing number of gatekeepers who are uniformly clothed in green'. Faulkner goes on to describe how 'the great south walk is crowded in spring and summer with a display of all the beauty and fashion of the great metropolis'. The painter Benjamin Robert Haydon, writing in the 1850s, adored the gardens Caroline had created: 'Here in Kensington are some of the most poetical bits of trees ... and sunny brown and green glens and tawny earth.'

The round of life at Kensington – and we must remember that Kensington was still a small countryside village in the early eighteenth century – consisted of the king's levee in the morning, to which only friends and important ministers were admitted, followed by a more general crowd in the drawing room later in the morning, dinner at around 3 p.m. (eating late in the evening is a modern concept), then a walk in the gardens and the all-important cards in the evening.

By the late 1730s, with the departure of Frederick and his entourage, Kensington Palace became the principal home of Frederick's five sisters – 'principal' home because inevitably, in keeping with their status as royal children, they moved between palaces a fair bit, as their mother and father did.

Three of the sisters, Anne, Mary and Louisa, finally left Kensington in the 1740s when they went abroad to marry foreign princes, but Caroline and Amelia stayed on with their increasingly bad-tempered, ageing father.

Also in residence was Prince William, Duke of Cumberland ('Butcher Cumberland'), the princesses' brother; the Duke of Grafton (who was also Lord Chamberlain); Mistress of the Robes (and royal mistress) Henrietta Howard – who in 1734 was finally given permission to retire to Twickenham – and of course Caroline's favourite, John, Lord Hervey. In addition, there were a number of courtiers who came, stayed for a time, got nowhere and disappeared.

But the sense that Kensington was a home for lesser royals was increasing and with the death of Caroline in 1737, Kensington began its decline from primary royal residence to 'aunt heap' and home to hangers-on, eccentrics and elderly retainers.

In his widowhood, George II, his two remaining daughters and his mistress Amalie von Wallmoden continued to live at Kensington – in fact, George spent more time at Kensington after his wife died than he ever did before. As age crept upon him, he visited Hanover less often. Aged seventy-six – a remarkable age for the time – he died, in his lavatory at Kensington from a ruptured aortic aneurism. His physician Frank Nicholls reported how a servant heard George enter the royal lavatory at his usual time and then heard a sigh 'which was not quite the usual royal wind'. He rushed in and found the king unconscious on the floor. Worse, he had hit his head on a bureau as he fell. He was carried to his bed but was already dead. When he was buried in Westminster Abbey it was noted that one side of his late wife's coffin was missing; the opposite side of George's coffin was also missing so that once side by side, their dust would mingle.

This was the gentler, more sensitive side of George. But the harsher side had never gone away, and he had never reconciled with his son. As previously noted, he was apparently delighted when Frederick predeceased him in 1751. Upon his own death, therefore, the crown passed to Frederick's eldest son, who became George III.

With the death of George II, Kensington ceased for ever to be the home of the monarch and the court. The magnificent state rooms were slowly allowed to decay until they became a dilapidated store for coal, broken furniture and old pictures.

Meanwhile, the rest of the palace began a long cyclical period during which various apartments were updated and modernised, then left to fall apart before being renovated once more. No longer wanted by the immediate royal family, Kensington became home to a seemingly endless stream of odd uncles, distant cousins, retired courtiers and down-at-heel aristocrats. Birth gave them innate privileges and a luxurious lifestyle that no one was to question for another century and a half.

CHAPTER SEVEN

CHANGE AND DECAY

'Lord Chancellor, did I deliver the speech well?
I am glad of that for there was nothing in it.'
GEORGE III

George III (1738–1820) came to the throne in 1760 aged just twenty-two. It is easy to imagine that his memories of Kensington were not entirely happy, so it was no surprise when he decided he preferred Buckingham House (later Buckingham Palace), which he had bought and had rebuilt in 1762.

A stickler for correct behaviour, George III was famously devoted to his wife, Queen Charlotte – unlike his grandfather and great-grandfather, he never took a mistress – but he produced an heir who was probably the most eccentric and immoral monarch Britain has ever had to put up with. George IV was the complete opposite of his father; where George III had no mistresses, his son had a dozen or more; where George III centred his life on his wife and family, George IV married a Catholic (apparently illegally), then married a German relative he hated and then tried to divorce. Given his highly moralistic parents, George IV was yet another example, admittedly in a new guise, of that old Hanoverian trope: the rebellious heir.

George IV could never really understand why he was so hated by his subjects, but hated he was. The problem was that, both as regent and as king, he was a deeply frivolous, greedy, childish character who cared only for his own pleasure. At a time when the British economy was in deep trouble, he spent colossal amounts of money on anything and everything that took his fancy. His subjects mocked his bloated, obese appearance and most of all his treatment of his wife, Caroline of Brunswick (1768–1821).

George IV slept with his wife only once (or possibly three times – the records vary) and his aversion to her was based, according to George, anyway, on the fact that she did not wash.

So, the couple separated only days after they had married and Caroline was packed off (or packed herself off) to various houses – one in Bayswater, west London, another in south London and more often than not to an apartment at Kensington Palace which was kept for her use.

And it was here that her eccentricity really flourished – she caused a scandal, for example, by insisting on receiving visitors in the morning before she was dressed; on warm days she would wander into the gardens, which were by then open to the public, and talk to anyone who happened along. Her lack of formality and insistence that she would talk to anyone and everyone was a trait echoed by Diana, Princess of Wales, in the very same park almost two centuries later.

Within a year of their ill-fated marriage, in 1796 Caroline gave birth to George IV's only legitimate child, who was christened Charlotte Augusta. George finally escaped from Caroline – not because he divorced her, but because she died aged just fifty-three – in 1821. He had been king for only a year.

His daughter Princess Charlotte Augusta of Wales was immensely popular and might easily have expected to become queen following the death of her father, but she died in childbirth aged just twenty-one in 1817. When her father died in 1830, a constitutional crisis loomed as the surviving sons of George III – famously characterised by Queen Victoria as the wicked uncles – had numerous illegitimate children but not a single legitimate one between them. This was a serious threat to the future of the House of Hanover.

CHAPTER EIGHT

ANCESTRAL VICES

'A man lowers himself by frequenting the society of Germans ... I can no longer abide this race with which a man is always in bad company.'
FRIEDRICH NIETZSCHE

Whenever Victoria looked back at her forebears, she shuddered. She found the morals of her grandfather George III's sons deeply repugnant; she hated their immoral lives, their endless mistresses and illegitimate children. She hated almost everything they stood for. She was determined that her nine children would grow up in an environment of strict morality – her resolve in this respect actually mirrored that of her grandfather George III, who, as we have seen, took no mistresses and was devoted to his family. George III's moralistic regime created a gross sensualist in the Prince Regent, who was to become George IV; nearly eighty years later, Queen Victoria and Prince Albert produced Edward VII, who was in many ways remarkably similar to his great-uncle the Prince Regent – grossly overweight, self-indulgent, promiscuous and, according to many, completely lacking in any moral sense.

For sixty years after George III decided not to base his court at Kensington, the palace slowly decayed. Walls bulged as the result of damp rising from the marshy ground; gradually the roof began to leak and birds nested in the rafters; the window glass cracked and was patched or left broken. There were still tenants – including one or two surviving children of George III – and it is easy to imagine them walking carefully along the dusty corridors avoiding the buckets set to catch the drips from the ceiling.

With their cocooned lives, the inhabitants of Kensington Palace in the nineteenth century were as disconnected from reality as their modern counterparts. A servant who worked at Kensington Palace in the 1960s explains that even then, the tenants were completely unaware of what was necessary to prevent the building collapsing around them.

They had absolutely no idea about repairs and maintenance, no practical sense at all. They had grown up in a world where people who were essentially invisible to them did all the work – cleaning, mending window sashes, fixing slates that had slipped on the roof. I remember when a large part of the window glass in one room cracked and then fell out in a room occupied by Princess Alice of Athlone [the last surviving grandchild of Queen Victoria]. It was winter but Alice just sat there with the freezing wind whistling around her ears until someone turned up to fix it. She had been brought up, I imagine, not to notice such things – they were beneath the dignity of a royal. Or there might be another kinder explanation, I suppose – like most royals at that time she was a little batty, and she may not even have noticed and just thought it was a colder day than usual.

So, even if Kensington Palace was neglected, it was never empty and many of those who lived there in the immediate years after the court moved away were, like Alice in more recent times, decidedly eccentric. It was almost as if Caroline of Brunswick, with her pumpkin hat and refusal to wash, had become the archetype of so many future palace inhabitants.

Queen Victoria was born at Kensington Palace in 1819, just two years before the death of Caroline of Brunswick.

There is some dispute about the room in which she was born, but we know she was baptised by the Archbishop of Canterbury in the Cupola Room. The magnificent long gallery built for Queen Anne had been subdivided into three by the time Victoria needed a playroom. In her diaries she also records that one of the smaller rooms created out of the gallery became her sitting room.

For all her later complaints about her miserable childhood, we know that her sitting room and bedroom were filled with the sort of toys most nineteenth-century children would hardly dare dream about – her mother bought her toys from the then famous Izzard of Upper Brook Street. Sets of marbles, a magnificent doll's house and 132 small wooden dolls known as peg dolls, a beautifully made toy carriage – all these survived and are still in the Royal Collection. In addition to her toys, the young princess also had a parrot and other caged birds.

Victoria's mother, the Duchess of Kent, may not have been obvious-ly eccentric, but she was controlling to an almost insane extent. Like many members of the royal family both then and now the duchess felt she could do no wrong. It was this intransigence that led to a permanent rift with the king.

Victoria's uncle William IV, who succeeded George IV (another uncle) in 1830, grew increasingly angry with the duchess for keeping his niece away from him. He suspected the duchess's motives, assuming – quite rightly – that she was determined to become regent in the event that he should die before Victoria reached the age of eighteen. Indeed, he openly declared that he was determined to survive long enough to keep the duchess out.

The Duchess of Kent ignored all William's complaints and demands that Victoria be allowed to come to court more often. She may have assured herself that she was keeping Victoria from the moral cesspit that William and his brothers represented; she may even have convinced herself that she was carefully training her daughter to become queen, but the truth was different. William's suspicions were well founded – the duchess would indeed become regent if William died too soon, and she would reign with the help of her friend and confidant Sir John Conroy, an Irish aristocrat who seemed able to rule the duchess as much as the duchess ruled her daughter, Victoria.

For the plan to work, the duchess felt it was essential that Victoria be kept well away from her uncles, especially King William, not because their moral influence might be unwelcome but rather so that the young woman would acquiesce in all her mother's wishes.

Things came to a head when, having invited the seventeen-year-old Victoria and her mother to a dinner at Windsor – an invitation to celebrate the queen's birthday could not easily be refused – William made a speech in which he angrily criticised the duchess; indeed, one suspects that he invited her with the sole purpose of attacking her.

It seems that, obsessed with the idea that she might one day rule, the duchess had taken over far more rooms at Kensington Palace than had originally been agreed and she had done so without asking William. He was apoplectic with rage and determined to give her a dressing-down. In the moment of greeting the young Victoria at Windsor he apparently looked across at her mother, whom he had studiously ignored until then, and said that 'an unwarrantable liberty' had been taken with one of his palaces and that he 'neither understood nor would endure conduct so disrespectful'. The king was genuinely angry, but not at the fact of the duchess commandeering a greater part of one of his palaces – that was for him a mere symbol of a deeper disrespect; it was, if you like, a symbol of her desire to supplant him.

It was 1836 and in less than a year, Victoria would be old enough to rule without a regent. The king drove home his message. With the duchess just yards away he stood up in front of the assembled courtiers and said that if he managed to live another year, he:

> should then have the satisfaction of leaving the royal authority to the personal exercise of that young lady, the heiress presumptive of the crown, and not in the hands of the person now near me, who is surrounded by evil advisers and who is herself incompetent to act with propriety in the station in which she would be placed. I have no hesitation in saying I have been insulted – grossly and continually insulted by that person.

The duchess's reaction was to sit stony-faced. Of course, not everyone would have taken the speech seriously, as even William's greatest friends would not have described him as astute or reasonable. Indeed, he was described as 'cracked' by the diarist Charles Greville and it was commonly accepted that he was also a tantrum-prone buffoon. In this respect he was just like his father, grandfather and great-grandfather. For all her dislike of her Hanoverian forebears, Victoria did inherit at least one of their characteristics – throughout her life she was prone to violent tantrums.

From the day of her birth, Victoria's life was closely regulated. She later described her childhood as 'rather melancholy'. What is remarkable is that despite being kept away from the world until she was eighteen, she was never allowed to be alone for even a minute. She developed into a strong-minded, forceful woman who was actually very difficult to manage. But this is a truism, perhaps, of child-rearing – those with controlling parents may be rebellious as children, before becoming controlling as parents themselves.

Kept almost permanently at Kensington Palace, she was allowed to see her nurse, Mrs Brock; Mrs Strode, the housekeeper; and her governess, Louise Lehzen. At night her mother insisted on sleeping in the same room as Victoria, who was never allowed to walk in the gardens or even down the stairs unaccompanied. None of the stair-cases at Kensington Palace appear particularly dangerous, but during Victoria's childhood there seems to have been an absolute conviction – certainly in the mind of her mother – that if she was allowed to walk down them alone, she would fall. And so, this was never allowed. Amid all this nonsense, Victoria's one ally was Louise Lehzen.

Like her Hanoverian predecessors, Victoria perpetuated the family tradition of dysfunctionality; her own oddities and bizarre behaviour were to echo those of the ancestors whose influence she tried so hard to escape. Much later in life, her mourning for her dead husband Albert was so intense and long-lasting that her advisers thought she must have inherited her grandfather George III's insanity. And this view is understandable when one combines the obsession with mourning with Victoria's other eccentricities – she collected dead flowers from the graves of deceased royals, for example; she hated her eldest son (just as George I and George II had hated theirs).

That's not to say, however, that those marrying into Victoria's family were any less eccentric. Her relatives in Germany – a country to which she looked as the source of all things good – seemed equally odd. In 1866, for example, Queen Victoria's rather plain third daughter Helena was finally found a suitable German husband. He was Prince Christian of Schleswig-Holstein. When summoned to England to meet the princess, he convinced himself that he had actually been asked to marry the widowed Victoria. Undaunted, he acknowledged his mistake, married, and spent the rest of his life shooting and collecting glass eyes. His first glass eye had been bought to replace an eye lost in a shooting accident, but he became obsessed with them and had a large collection; he insisted they were all absolutely essential as he needed a different one for every occasion. He would take them out to show people at every dance, party and dinner engagement. He was known as 'glass eye bore'.

But such lunacy was a long way ahead of the young princess as she negotiated her way through those early years at Kensington.

CHAPTER NINE

THE PURITAN PARTY

'The queen is most anxious to enlist everyone in checking this mad,
wicked folly of "Women's Rights". It is a subject which makes
the queen so furious that she cannot contain herself.'

QUEEN VICTORIA

It was only by extraordinary chance that Victoria became queen at all. Her immediate predecessor, William IV, had ten illegitimate children but no heir.

William represented everything she later deplored and her loathing for him and her other 'wicked uncles' only intensified after she married Prince Albert of Saxe-Coburg and Gotha (1819–61) and chose to identify with the morbid puritanism of him and his Coburg relations.

But if William was bad, the brother he succeeded, George IV, was worse. One of the most hated of all the British monarchs, he separated from his wife Caroline of Brunswick, as we have seen, in such a vicious and vindictive way that almost overnight he turned her into one of the most popular figures in the country. Another brother, the Duke of

Cumberland, was worse again: a sadist who almost certainly murdered his own valet, he married a woman who was thought to have killed her previous two husbands.

Apart from Victoria's father, the Duke of Kent, only one of George III's sons had a legitimate heir. This, as we have seen, was Charlotte, Princess of Wales, who died in childbirth – a death that caused much consternation. Charlotte's bereaved husband Leopold throws a wonderfully absurd light on how royalty sometimes works: some years after the death of his wife, finding himself at a loose end, he was offered the throne of both Belgium and Greece to choose from, rather as one might be offered tea or coffee. He chose Belgium.

But with the death of Charlotte, all of George III's middle-aged sons sprang into action, partly encouraged by the promise of money from the British government if they would agree to leave their mistresses, marry someone suitable and try to father an heir.

Victoria's father, the Duke of Kent, immediately did as he was told. Notoriously in need of money, he dumped his mistress, the French actress Julie de Saint Laurent – whom he'd been with for twenty-seven years – and married a German princess in the hopes of fathering the future heir to the British throne. By marrying, he also ensured a significant increase in his annual grant from the government.

His bride was Marie Luise Viktoria, Princess of Saxe-Coburg-Saalfeld. She was thirty-two and, by the standards of the day, it was seen as a long shot that she would conceive and bear an heir who would survive to adulthood, but that is exactly what she did. She was a widow with two children by her first husband. She might well have been considered past marriageable age under normal circumstances, but these were not normal circumstances. The appeal of the marriage for her was considerable – she was almost bankrupt, and marriage to the Duke of Kent, who could usually secure credit despite his own spendthrift ways, would at least secure her financial future.

Queen Victoria always boasted that she was the daughter of a soldier, but she rarely went into details, which is perhaps just as well as the Duke of Kent was as bad a soldier as it is possible to imagine. He first was posted to Gibraltar as an ordinary officer in 1790, having been disgraced after returning home from Geneva without leave that year, but wherever he served, he seems to have been hated by his soldiers for his sadism and brutality: he had his men flogged for even minor errors and omissions. Several men were flogged so badly that they died. In 1791, fearing a mutiny, the British government ordered him to Canada, largely because it was so far away that however badly he treated his soldiers, people in England were unlikely to hear about it. While in Canada he had a number of men sentenced to death for what seemed to many to be relatively trivial breaches of discipline. Despite his military failures at Gibraltar, the duke absolutely refused to listen to anyone who suggested his regime of floggings and executions might be unwise.

Finally, the government was forced to act to prevent a rebellion and – following a time in the West Indies – the duke was recalled to England. In a move that confirms the Hanoverian kings' tendency towards madness, George III sent him back to Gibraltar, but this time with even more power as Governor General. It was as if nothing had been learned from more than a decade of stupid decisions.

From the perspective of the early twenty-first century, it seems almost incredible that despite the evidence of the duke's extraordinary incompetence, the fact of his royal birth meant that a military role had to be found for him. In the end, even his royal birth was not enough – when a mutiny (hatched among his own men in Gibraltar) began in 1803, he was recalled and his career finally came to an end. He was just thirty-five. That Victoria seems to have been proud of her father's soldiering speaks volumes about the eccentricities of the royal family. He spent the rest of his life complaining that he was a perfectly decent man who had been badly treated. And if he was blind to his own military shortcomings, this was nothing compared to his refusal to acknowledge his financial ones. When, despite his enormous income, he ran up debts of more than £200,000, that too was the fault of others and he was indignant when the king refused to pay off his debts. He was, in modern parlance, the most spoiled of spoiled brats.

As one of his first biographers, the broadly sympathetic Roger Fulford, put it:

> He had nothing in his character ... to enable him to face misfortune. As a youth he had firmly believed that everything conspired to make a prince's path through the world easy and glorious ... When disaster overtook him, he could not imagine that it might be himself who was to blame.

Some idea of his extravagance – an extravagance he believed was his right – can be gained from the following account of his house at Ealing. We know all his houses were run along similar lines, so we can be fairly sure that what applied in Ealing also applied to his apartments at Kensington Palace. Roger Fulford writes:

> The happiest time for the Duke ... was at Castle Hill Lodge, a pleasant,

low house surrounded by forty acres of parkland. There was a winding drive up to the house which the Duke kept brilliantly lighted at night, every night throughout the year … There was a system of bells from the porter's lodge at the entrance gates up to the house so that there were always six footmen standing at the front door when anyone called. Inside there were scores of menservants, always with new liveries, their hair perfectly dressed and powdered by a resident hairdresser who was kept for the purpose. Every morning each servant had to present himself before the Duke to show that he was perfectly dressed and clean.

In the sitting rooms there were bell ropes all along the walls, each of which summoned a particular servant. The Duke always got up at six and a fire had to be lit for him at five. One servant therefore stayed up all night and slept only during the day so there should be no danger of the fire not being lighted. The house was filled with musical devices, cages of artificial singing birds, organs with dancing horses, and musical clocks. At night the corridors – all the corridors – and halls were lighted with hundreds of coloured lights.

The curious thing about the duke is that as well as being 'a violent sadistic lunatic' (Fulford again), he also had a reputation for personal kindness and for taking an interest in the welfare of the poor. He even befriended trade unionist founder Robert Owen and took an interest in his work. On the other hand, the duke was so greedy for money throughout his life – money he no sooner had in his pocket than he spent it – that he even borrowed money from Owen and made sure he never repaid it. And all this despite an income from the British taxpayer of £12,000 a year (more than £1 million in 2020), a sum he considered insufficient.

Apologists for the duke tend to emphasise his kindness and the fact that he had kept the same mistress for twenty-seven years before being tempted by money and prestige into marrying. Others might have said, with some justification, that the duke would have sold his soul for a little extra cash. He told the MP Thomas Creevey that he expected his income from the British government to increase to at least £25,000 annually, as that was the amount that had been settled on his brother Frederick, the Duke of York. He dismissed criticisms of his spendthrift ways and huge debts. When criticised for running up these debts, he insisted that 'the nation on the contrary is greatly my debtor', although of course he did not say why.

So, this was the man who won the race among the ageing sons of George III to provide an heir to the British throne. When his wife became pregnant in 1818, the couple had recently begun living in Amorbach, Germany, rather than at Kensington – partly, no doubt, to avoid the duke's creditors.

A few months later, determined the child should be born in England, the duke left Amorbach for Kensington Palace. And if there was very little amusing about Victoria's solemn, puritanical reign, there was certainly much to amuse about her journey, *in utero*, as it were, to London.

As A. N. Wilson points out in his 2014 biography of Victoria, when the royal couple left Germany in March 1819, they didn't even have enough money to tip a coachman, so the duke drove the coach himself.

But it should not be imagined that the Duke and his wife travelled in a broken-down old coach – in fact, the duke drove the first carriage, containing his by now heavily pregnant wife, while behind came a coach containing the duke's stepdaughter Feodore and her favourite cats, dogs and songbirds; and behind that coach came other vehicles carrying servants including a cook and a doctor. Also perched inside the coach was Sir John Conroy, the duke's equerry: a man who was to spend the next two decades trying to control and manipulate Victoria and her household for his own ends.

Conroy seems to have laboured under the illusion – and it almost certainly was an illusion – that his wife was the illegitimate daughter of the man for whom he was working. In other words, he was convinced, according to evidence unearthed by Conroy's biographer Katherine Hudson, that his wife was Victoria's half-sister, though why this should have made him obsessive in his desire to be the power behind the throne when Victoria came of age is still a mystery. Perhaps it was simply that, to paraphrase J. R. R. Tolkien, 'All men desire power', and as their proximity to power increases, so too does their desire for it.

The journey to London – more than 400 miles – must have been extraordinarily difficult, on rough roads, in a badly sprung coach with a heavily pregnant woman, but at least it was spring. Having started their journey on 28 March, they reached Calais on 18 April only to find the Channel too rough for a crossing. Almost a week later the sea – still by no means calm – allowed the party to embark at last.

Emotionally and spiritually Victoria always thought of herself as German – in later life she always referred to 'dear Germany', and she insisted that all her children should learn the language – but at the time her mother reached Kensington Palace after that bumpy journey along the muddy roads of Europe, the British royal family's connection to various German principalities was far more substantial. For the Hanoverians and their families, England was perhaps just another province, albeit a wealthy and influential one. None of the Georges had ever given up their titles to the land of their origin – George II, for example, never stopped being Duke of Brunswick-Lüneburg and a prince-elector of the Holy Roman Empire.

English royal palaces were therefore often heavily occupied by German relatives – plus their mistresses, servants and senior staff – so it is no surprise that the Prince Regent (who didn't become king until his father's death in 1820) was happy, as early as 1798, to offer his brother the Duke of Kent an apartment at Kensington Palace, and it was to this same apartment that he returned with his pregnant wife in 1819.

The apartment was large and, according to some sources, it was later expanded to include a number of rooms formerly occupied by the Prince Regent's hated wife, Caroline of Brunswick, who had enjoyed the run of nearly fifty rooms in total until 1814, when she left England for good.

Partly because Kensington had been allowed to slumber for so long – and no doubt partly because the Prince Regent was reluctant to spend money on a building that housed his wife – much of the Duke of Kent's apartment was in a poor condition when he took it over in 1798. There were leaks in the roof, and many of the rooms had been partly repaired or refurbished but then left half-finished by workmen. And when Caroline left England in 1814, as a purely vindictive act against his wife, the Regent deliberately removed everything of interest and value from his wife's former apartment – there was virtually no furniture, and certainly no pictures, rugs, beds or, in some cases, even fireplaces.

Despite the £12,000-a-year income the Duke of Kent enjoyed and the fact that renowned architect James Wyatt had been employed – at the expense of the Treasury – to modernise his apartment, Kent never seems to have been satisfied that his rooms were quite grand enough for a person of his importance. This was true when he took the rooms over in 1798, and it was still true when he returned from Germany with his pregnant wife two decades later.

Despite George III's insistence that any work done at Kensington for the duke should be plain and relatively inexpensive, from the moment he took possession of his apartment at Kensington in 1798 his brother ordered numerous improvements from James Wyatt that completely ignored budgetary considerations. It is true to an extent that costs rose because repairs were complicated by structural work that had nothing to do with the Duke of Kent – when an outer wall collapsed on one of Wren's original pavilions, for example, estimates from £6,000 to £10,000 were submitted to rebuild the wall.

Nevertheless, costs for non-necessary work continued to rise and the improvements never seemed to end – vast sums were spent on the latest wallpapers, hot water pipes (an early form of central heating upon which the duke insisted), costly carpets, desks and chairs for his two libraries, and a massive reordering of his rooms so that his servants would be less obvious when they were moving about. A new grand staircase was also built to provide a sufficiently imposing entrance to the duke's drawing room and dining room.

After twenty years of almost continuous work, the duke was still complaining when he left for Germany in 1818.

When he returned a year later with his pregnant wife, he was still obsessed with the need for alterations. He continued to protest about the apartment – and, even more vociferously, about his annual grant – right up to his death in 1820.

But at least the duke was allowed to live at Kensington. When, many years earlier, he had suggested that he be officially allowed to live there with his mistress Madame de Saint-Laurent, the king had forbidden it (although by then they had lived there together for some time) and so the duke had retreated to his house in Knightsbridge or to his house in Ealing or, when the tradesmen demanded their bills be paid, to Germany. Until he returned for good with his pregnant wife in 1819, Kensington had been used by the duke only when he wanted to berate the workmen, or for an occasional stopover.

The apartment to which the couple returned comprised most of the ground floor and first-floor rooms on the East Front and, after the initial redecorating on which the duke insisted, the couple settled down to await the birth, which by now was imminent.

Victoria was born at 4.15 a.m. on 24 May 1819 in a 'low-ceilinged room on the first floor', according to Ernest Law, writing in 1906. Less than a year later, her father the duke died from pneumonia aged just fifty-two.

Baron Stockmar (1787–1863), who was to exert such an influence over the future queen, wrote in his memoirs: 'A pretty little princess, plump as a partridge, was born. The Duke of Kent was delighted with his child and liked to show her constantly to his companions and intimate friends with the words, "Take care of her, for she will be Queen of England.'"

The duke wrote a rather cross letter to his chaplain after the chaplain had written to commiserate that the child had not been a boy. The duke wrote:

> As to the circumstance of that child not proving to be a son instead of a daughter, I feel it due to myself to declare that such sentiments are not in unison with my own; for I am decidedly of opinion that the decrees of Providence are at all times wisest and best.

Historical record seems to fall silent for a while after this, but in the summer of 1820 the politician and anti-slavery campaigner William Wilberforce (1759–1833) visited the Duchess of Kent at Kensington. On 21 July of that year he wrote: 'She received me this morning with her fine animated child on the floor by her side, with its playthings of which I soon became one.'

Of course, in Victoria's early years no sense of imprisonment or harshness would have encroached upon what was an indisputably gilded upbringing. Unlike millions of British children, she had the finest food, a warm dry bed, toys and the best possible care, especially from her devoted governess, Baroness Louise Lehzen. Lehzen, who was summoned from Hanover when Victoria was five, became more important to Victoria than her mother. George IV hated the idea that any commoner should live in close proximity to his niece, so, in 1827, he solved the problem at a stroke by making Lehzen a baroness.

The historian Ernest Law, who had spoken to people who had known Kensington Palace during this period, wrote in 1900: 'Most of the future queen's early years were passed at Kensington Palace in great privacy and retirement', yet she was never permitted to be alone – not even for a moment.

What Law doesn't say – as, like most Victorian commentators and historians, he is nothing if not discreet – is that Victoria was held a virtual prisoner by her mother. For years after she became queen, Victoria blamed her mother for her 'melancholy' childhood, but in her middle years she came to believe that her mother had also been to some extent a victim: suffering at the hands of the arch-villain Sir John Conroy, who seems to have stalked the corridors at Kensington like the dark antagonist of a Victorian melodrama.

Though she saw little that was good in her upbringing, Victoria seems to have absorbed a controlling, puritanical attitude not unlike her mother's; an attitude that led ultimately to the sombre, repressed, hypocritical moral agenda of the Victorian era in which, legend has it, even table legs had to be covered.

Later on, in her private life with her husband Albert, Victoria was anything but prudish; numerous historians have emphasised that, judging by her letters and journals, Victoria delighted in her physical relationship with her husband and was not repressed in the least. After her first night as Albert's wife she wrote in her journal:

It was a gratifying and bewildering experience ... I never, never spent such an evening. His excessive love and affection gave me feelings of heavenly love and happiness. He clasped me in his arms and we kissed each other again and again.

His beauty, his sweetness and gentleness — really how can I ever be thankful enough to have such a husband!

To lie by his side, and in his arms, and on his dear bosom, and be called by names of tenderness, I have never yet heard used to me before — this was the happiest day of my life. It was bliss beyond belief!

When day dawned (for we did not sleep much) and I beheld that beautiful face by my side, it was more than I can express! Oh, was ever woman so blessed as I am.

A few months later Victoria sent Albert an erotic painting that remains under lock and key in the Royal Collection.

Despite her subsequent reputation, Victoria was not actually that different from her sex-crazed uncles, and it is easy to believe that had she been a man her appetites would not have been restrained by marriage. A passionate nature was a major part of her Hanoverian inheritance, but it was combined with rigid self-discipline and an unyielding determination to control both her husband and her children. Her desire for control – passed down from her mother – led to blistering rows with her husband and unhappiness for her children, especially the Prince of Wales; and falling out with one's heir, as we have seen, was most definitely a Hanoverian trait.

Over a period of more than twenty years, Victoria's journals were edited and transcribed by her youngest daughter, Princess Beatrice, who destroyed anything and everything that did not fit the image of the old queen that the family wished to perpetuate – if Beatrice had merely transcribed the journals verbatim, she might have kept the originals, but of the 122 original books in which Victoria had written her journals, Beatrice destroyed all but fourteen.

We know the kind of thing Beatrice removed because Reginald Brett, Viscount Esher, had been given permission to copy extracts from the original diaries for a book he was writing long before Beatrice edited them. He included a line in which Victoria describes Albert helping her put her stockings on before breakfast. In Beatrice's version of the same extract the line about the stockings has vanished.

The most significant passages to be cut, however, focused on Victoria's passion for her Scottish gillie, John Brown. Her comments about Brown must have seemed to emulate the desires of those 'wicked uncles', so they were destroyed – even fairly innocent remarks about Brown were taken out.

As a child we know Victoria was capable of what she described herself in her earliest journals as 'violent feelings of affection'. There is no reason to believe that these violent affections did not attach themselves, later in life, to John Brown and other men.

What remains in Beatrice's version of the diaries is fairly anodyne, but it does at least reveal the lighter side of the young princess's life at Kensington. Take the following entry from Wednesday 1 January 1834:

I awoke at 7. Mamma gave me a scrap-book, an annual, and three German almanacks. I gave her a painting and drawing done by me, two rubbed screens, an annual, some New Year's Wishes, and a nosegay. Lehzen gave me two lovely china jars for matches, a beautiful little pastille-burner, and two New Year's Wishes. Mamma gave her a poplin dress, a black velvet muff, and a cup. I gave her, a German almanack, a pair of sisars [*sic*] a drawing done by me, some New Year's Wishes, and a memorandum book. At 9 we breakfasted. After breakfast Mamma gave me some prints and costumes and a lovely footstool of her own work. And later too she gave me some beautiful outlines by Retzch of Schiller's poem 'Pegasus im Joche'. At 12 we went out walking and came home at 1. At 1 we lunched. At 3 came Victoire till 6. At 7 we went to dine at the Conroys. After dinner came Aunt Sophia. I stayed there till ½ past 9. I was soon in bed and asleep.

Victoria's later sense that life was gloomy at Kensington may well have stemmed from her mother's early anxieties – Victoria was only a small child when her father died, after all.

Victoria's parents had been staying at Sidmouth in Devon for the sea air – something of a twentieth-century obsession – when the duke died suddenly, and when the distraught duchess eventually returned to London she discovered that all of her husband's possessions had been removed from Kensington and sold to pay his huge debts.

'Poverty' for a duchess was a very different experience from poverty for someone lower down the social scale but she would have been shocked and worried by the sudden change in her circumstances. However, she quickly borrowed enough money to buy back everything that had been sold from the Kensington apartment – there is something almost farcical in the idea of tons of furniture and pictures being carted out of the palace one week only to be carted back in again a few weeks later.

As the mother of the heir to the throne, the duchess did not have to wait long for the government to step in: she was offered a large annual payment of £12,000, supplemented by £3,000 a year from Victoria's

Uncle Leopold – that same uncle who had so casually accepted the throne of Belgium.

The duchess's financial worries may have been over, but she had other troubles, not least of which was the fact that she could hardly speak any English – a kind of siege mentality seems to have set in, as she felt isolated and unsure in a country in which she had lived for such a short time. She was always likely to be vulnerable to a confident, worldly figure – and that figure was Sir John Conroy. He had been her husband's equerry, but after the duke's death he quickly became a sort of Svengali to the duchess.

Before Victoria was a year old, George III, mostly considered 'mad' for the latter part of his reign, finally died and the Prince Regent became George IV. He had heartily disliked his brother, the Duke of Kent, but he could hardly evict the duchess and her daughter Victoria from Kensington, much though he might have wanted to. So the duchess and her daughter stayed on, living in the same rooms they had used during the duke's lifetime. But with something of her husband's obsession for altering, enlarging and constantly updating, the duchess oversaw a continual stream of workmen over the next seventeen years and more. And for those seventeen years Victoria remained carefully supervised under what came to be known as the Kensington System – a system whose key elements were isolation and separation from the rest of the royal family.

It is difficult not to sympathise, to some extent, with the Duchess of Kent's determination to keep her daughter away from George IV – after all, she had seen him in action, as it were, when George had invited his niece and her mother to Windsor to meet Victoria's aunt the Queen of Württemberg. During dinner, the Duchess of Kent would have noticed – as indeed the nine-year-old Victoria would – that the king was absolutely smitten by Victoria's half-sister, Feodore, who was then just eighteen. The old king, obese and gouty, was sixty-four, yet, according to some historians, he went out of his way to give the impression he might marry Feodore. It may have been just a rumour, but in any event the Duchess of Kent must have been horrified.

Luckily, the king's chief mistress, Lady Conyngham (the mother of the man who, nearly a decade later, was to travel to Kensington to tell Victoria she was queen), saw what was happening and sent the Duchess of Kent, Feodore and Victoria straight back to Kensington. But the encounter seemed to crystallise all of the duchess's fears about the corrupting influence of the English court.

The apartment at Kensington in which Victoria and her mother lived changed considerably over the years but always included a dressing room, dining room, drawing room, a room known as the Crimson Room and the South Bedroom, where Princess Victoria slept. Their apartment ran along the East Front and part of the South Front on the first floor. There was a library on the ground floor and here too were most of the rooms used by the servants, including a footman, a cook, a secretary and a number of maids.

Some of the furniture bought back by the duchess after her husband's death had not originally been paid for by the duke – indeed, a number of manufacturers were still trying to get paid after Victoria's accession in 1837! It was a badge of honour among royalty that debts could be ignored.

꙰

But what was day-to-day life at Kensington like for the young Victoria?

Writing in *Old and New London*, published in 1878, Edward Walford described seeing the young Victoria playing in Kensington Gardens. He saw her 'skipping[ing] along between her mother and sister, the princess Feodore, holding a hand of each'.

She was allowed to walk with her dog, Dash, in Kensington Gardens – as long as she was accompanied.

Writing in *The Old Court Suburb*, published in 1855, Leigh Hunt recalled, 'I saw her [Princess Victoria] coming up a cross path from the Bayswater gate with a girl of her own age by her side.'

This was not the Baroness Lehzen, who was a good deal older, but Princess Feodore, her half-sister and greatest friend in these early years. Hunt noted that Victoria held Feodore's hand 'as if she loved'. He noted too that wherever the princess wandered, behind her came 'a magnificent footman in scarlet'.

Walking may have appealed to Victoria, but she much preferred to explore the gardens in a tiny cart pulled by a carefully trained goat; when she grew bigger the cart was exchanged for a larger model pulled by a donkey. As a young teenager Victoria progressed to a phaeton – a small, sporty open carriage – pulled by two ponies, but no doubt she used first one carriage and then another to add variety to what must have sometimes seemed very dull days.

Writing many decades later, Richard Holmes, the Queen's Librarian, also recalled the princess's childhood routine in his book *Queen Victoria*, first published in 1897. Like every biographer and memoirist prior to Lytton Strachey in the 1920s, Holmes saw no

reason to portray the princess in anything other than a flattering light.
He writes:

> During those early years and before a regular course of study had been
> attempted, the family life at the palace was simple and regular. Breakfast
> was served in summer at 8 a.m., the princess Victoria having her bread
> and milk and fruit on a little table at her mother's side. After breakfast
> the princess Feodore studied with her governess and the princess Vic-
> toria went out for a drive or a walk in the park.
>
> It has been said that at this time she was instructed by her mother,
> but this is not the case as the duchess never gave her daughter any
> lessons. At 2 p.m. there was a plain dinner. In the afternoon, another
> walk or drive. At the time of her mother's dinner, the princess had her
> supper laid at her side. At 9 p.m. she retired to her bed, which was
> placed close to her mother's.

If this really was her routine, and it varied as little as she later complained, then it is perhaps no wonder that she felt her early years were
stultifying and melancholy. However, it does seem that she received a
well-rounded education by the standards of the day.

By the age of five she was being taught dancing, singing, drawing
and painting – Victoria painted hundreds of rather good watercol-
ours – and French. German, which she already knew, was not allowed.
English was insisted upon for everyday use – presumably memories of
early monarchs being mocked for their German accents were upper-
most in her mother's mind. She also had riding lessons in the park and
riding was to be a lifelong passion along with letter writing and, above
all else, compiling her journal. She kept a journal for more than five

years at Kensington Palace, from the age of thirteen until she ascended the throne – and she was still writing in her journal ten days before she died in 1901.

In his *Recollections*, the Duke of Albemarle remembered a morning spent at Kensington Palace. He happened to look out of a window on the first floor one morning and saw the princess, aged seven: 'She was in the habit of watering the plants immediately under the window. It was amusing to see how impartially she divided the contents of the watering pot between the plants and her own feet…'

The author Charles Knight, while strolling through Kensington Gardens one weekday morning in 1828, recalled seeing the young Victoria: 'As I passed along the broad central walk, I saw a group on the lawn before the palace … The duchess and her daughter were breakfasting in the open air.' Knight's observations reveal the remarkable reality that at this time members of the royal family were not obsessed with privacy and security as they are now. Just as Charles II and earlier monarchs had been obliged to appear in public, walking among their subjects, attended by anyone who happened to wish to join the party, so Victoria and her mother thought nothing of being on view. They knew, as modern royals sometimes forget, that the royal family is to some extent public property; it is the price they pay for being bankrolled by the state.

The great nineteenth-century novelist Sir Walter Scott – whose books Victoria later devoured – dined at Kensington Palace one evening when the princess was nine. He did not note the pleasant strolls in the garden that others had, and his comments reflect the darker side of life inside the palace. 'This little lady is educated,' he recalled, 'with much care and watched so closely that no busy maid has a moment to whisper, "You are heir of England"…'

Few early observers mention Victoria's passionate nature, nor that it had a deeply negative side. Like her grandfather, her great-grandfather and her uncles, she was subject to violent outbursts – the kind of explosions and tantrums that we would now associate with a dysfunctional upbringing. Her violent temper was remarkably reminiscent of George II's occasional rages – as we have seen, when thwarted he would hurl his wig to the ground and then kick it around in front of the whole court. Victoria regularly stormed and stamped, once even throwing a pair of scissors at her governess, Louise Lehzen. A tendency towards fury was something she also handed on to her son and heir Albert, later Edward VII.

Louise Lehzen was born in 1784, the daughter of a German clergyman, and the fact that she became such a dominant figure in Victoria's life at Kensington Palace can be attributed entirely to her personal qualities. She seems to have been almost as controlling as Victoria's mother, but she had a warm quality that sweetened the bitter pill. But her influence did not go unnoticed.

She had started work at Kensington not as one of Victoria's attendants but as the governess of Victoria's half-sister, Feodore. She arrived at Kensington in 1819 and made such a difference to Feodore's education and general attitude that she was soon also assisting with Victoria's schooling, as well as helping her to control her rages by reading books out loud to her, sometimes as they strolled together in the gardens.

Victoria never fully learned to manage her emotions, but she grew fond of Lehzen and recognised her positive influence. They remained friends long after Lehzen left the palace; in fact, they were still on good terms when Lehzen died in 1870. When Albert insisted that Lehzen must be dismissed, she at least received the consolation prize of seeing Victoria in tears at the news.

Even as she lived her secluded life, Victoria would have been aware – if only from the whisperings of her mother, Conroy and Lehzen – that as the years passed, her chances of becoming queen were increasing dramatically. Still none of her uncles had produced an heir and with every passing year the likelihood of such an event became more remote; as we have seen, they were all well past their prime, to put it generously, and at least one – the Duke of Sussex, who was to live for decades at Kensington Palace – had no interest at all in joining the race to produce an heir.

Victoria was eleven when news reached Kensington Palace that her uncle George IV had died. As Ernest Law puts it, 'Only the life of William IV stood now between her and the throne.'

Louise Lehzen, it appears, was given the task of telling Victoria that she must prepare herself for the very real possibility of ascending the throne. Years later Louise wrote to Victoria reminding her of this momentous development: the letter was kept by Victoria and found among her papers when she died. She had annotated it, but her words agreed with those of her old governess. Lehzen describes how, with her future duty in mind, Victoria had been grateful that she had at least been well educated – she was especially grateful that Louise had taught her Latin.

Lehzen then goes on:

Some days previously I spoke to the Duchess of Kent, about the necessity, that now for the first time your Majesty ought to know your place in
the accession. Her royal highness agreed with me and I put the chron-
ological table in the historical book ... The princess opened the book
again and seeing the additional paper said, 'I never saw that before.'

'It was not thought necessary you should, Princess,' I answered. 'I
see I am nearer the throne than I thought.' 'So it is, madam,' I said.
After some moments the princess resumed, 'Now – many a child would
boast, but they don't know the difficulty; there is much splendour but
there is more responsibility...' The princess gave me again her hand
... I then said, 'But your Aunt Adelaide is still young and may have
children and they of course would ascend the throne after their father
William IV and not you Princess.' The princess answered, 'And if it
were so I should never feel disappointed for I know by the love Aunt
Adelaide bears me how fond she is of children...'

Of course, all this was designed by both Victoria and Lehzen to create
a sort of worthy myth of Victoria as an intensely humble, unassuming
young woman. It was almost certainly untrue, as no sooner did Victoria become queen than she exerted her power immediately and to
the full.

She reached eighteen, the age of maturity, on 24 May 1837. Less than
a month later William IV died. As soon as he had breathed his last –
he died at twelve minutes past two in the morning – the Archbishop
of Canterbury and the Lord Chamberlain, Frances Conyngham, leapt
into their carriages and set off for Kensington. Henry Conyngham, 1st

Marquess Conyngham, as we may recall, was the son of the late king's mistress. Elizabeth, Marchioness Conyngham, not only secured this lucrative appointment for her son but she also ensured her complaisant husband was given a peerage and money in return for not making a fuss about her infidelity. The Archbishop of Canterbury was William Howley (1766–1848), a man who was once attacked in the street for opposing parliamentary reform.

Howley must have been an extraordinary sight as he dashed up the great stairs at Kensington – he was well under five feet tall (as was Victoria) and towards the end of his life he insisted on wearing a wig despite the fact that wigs had been out of fashion for almost half a century.

When the two men arrived at Kensington, the Duchess of Kent, Victoria and everyone else was asleep. According to Frances Williams-Wynne, whose *Diaries of a Lady of Quality* was published more than twenty years later in 1864, the two men began hammering on the palace doors. 'They knocked, they thumped, they rang for a considerable time before they could rouse the porter. They were then left in an ante-room and forgotten. At last Victoria having dressed and reached them, they fell on their knees...'

By now the whole house would have been roused, the servants rushing here and there with the news. By nine o'clock that morning others began to arrive – first came the Prime Minister Lord Melbourne (1779–1848), then the Privy Councillors including the Duke of Wellington, and numerous bishops.

The new queen, no doubt in shock, apparently said little but smiled at each new visitor. Official visitors bowed deeply; members of her family went further and embraced the young queen. So far as we know this all took place in a small low-ceilinged room immediately below the Cube Room.

From everything that has been written about the queen, it seems that all the efforts her mother, Sir John Conroy and others went to in order to make Victoria easy to control actually had the opposite effect. Almost from the moment she became queen she knew that she had power and she was determined to exercise it. An immediate indication of her steely resolve came on that first morning as queen. She ordered the housekeeper Mrs Strode to prepare a room for her – until that day she had always shared a room with her mother.

What happened to Conroy and to her mother in the weeks that followed that morning in the little room at Kensington Palace showed that Victoria was now very much in charge.

CHAPTER TEN

OUT WITH THE DEVIL

'Conroy goes not to Court, the reason's plain
King John has played his part and ceased to reign.'
POPULAR SONG

Having spent so many years effectively in charge, Sir John Conroy expected to be allowed to kiss the new queen's hand that morning; he even dressed carefully in his apartments at Kensington especially for it. He proceeded along the corridors and up the stairs from his apartment to the Cupola Room, where Victoria was receiving her important visitors. It is not easy to imagine his rage and astonishment when, having arrived at the door and knocked, he was told that the new queen had given instructions stating that he was not to be admitted. In fact, Victoria absolutely refused to see him ever again, though no doubt she was aware of his presence, as he continued to be employed in her mother's household for some time. It was astonishingly decisive and ruthless, and it suggested that Victoria was going to be strong-minded and unforgiving.

Conroy immediately tried to limit the damage. He let it be known that the queen, while still Princess Victoria, had agreed that on her accession he should have the Order of the Bath and a pension of £3,000 a year. Both were refused, but Victoria cunningly asked the Prime Minister to convey the news to Conroy. Melbourne knew it would might look rather awkward if Conroy received nothing so he suggested that Conroy should be offered an Irish peerage – at the time considered greatly inferior to an English peerage, and one moreover that did not entitle the holder to a seat in the House of Lords. Conroy knew he was being fobbed off, refused the peerage and spent the rest of his life railing against those he thought had conspired against him.

He could not quite bring himself to insult the queen directly, but he must have been furious at being thwarted; his son, according to A. N. Wilson, blamed everything on 'that detestable bitch' Baroness Lehzen, conveniently forgetting that if Conroy had been less overbearing and dictatorial to Victoria the child, she might have smiled on him as Victoria the queen. But it was not to be.

But who was Sir John Conroy? We first met him bouncing along in that carriage on the journey from Germany to England with the Duke of Kent and his pregnant wife. Conroy was an Irishman by birth (strictly speaking, an Anglo-Irishman); a former soldier who, as we have seen, was equerry to the Duke of Kent. By the time that journey to England took place he had worked for the Kents for decades, married the daughter of the duke's aide-de-camp and accompanied his master halfway round the world.

After the Duke of Kent's death, Conroy's influence over the Duchess of Kent increased dramatically. He helped to devise the Kensington System that, looking back, Victoria so hated. And though she blamed her mother at least in part for the system, she always saw Conroy – perhaps too conveniently – as the villain of the piece. Indeed, as she grew older Conroy loomed ever larger in her demonology. He was probably not as bad as she later made out, but he was certainly over-confident and overbearing. Once secure in his belief in his influence over the Duchess of Kent and in his place at the centre of Kensington Palace life, he seems to have allowed power to go completely to his head – so much so that, having befriended Victoria's aunt, Princess Sophia (1777–1848), he helped himself to more than £18,000 of her money in order to buy an estate. It later transpired that he had also swindled the Duchess of Kent out of as much as £50,000.

Conroy seems to have suffered from a difficulty that was to beset Prince Albert and in more recent times Queen Elizabeth II's consort, Prince Philip, the Duke of Edinburgh. Until very recently – and many would say it persists to this day – powerful men have always assumed that the natural state of affairs is that men take the lead role rather than women. But what happens if the powerful man happens to be married to the reigning monarch? We know that both Prince Albert and the Duke of Edinburgh struggled to find a role in a world where their wives were the dominant partners.

Conroy's relationship with Victoria was similar in that he saw Victoria as a simple-minded girl who should be grateful to be led by an intelligent man of the world. Victoria's position as heir to the throne did not change the fact that, in his view, she was just an 'ignorant little child' and should therefore behave as he wished. Along with her mother, he really did fully expect to be the power behind the throne when she became queen.

Albert later behaved towards Victoria as Conroy had, and she fought back; both men found it difficult to reconcile their view of the natural inequality between men and women with the political realities. Indeed, Albert ultimately never managed to resign himself to reality, which is why his relationship with Victoria was so stormy. If Conroy brought out Victoria's steely resolve not to be controlled, then Albert – whom she had no wish to banish as she banished Conroy – brought out her temper tantrums.

The battle between Conroy and the Duchess of Kent on the one hand and Victoria on the other was played out in those lavish, dusty rooms at Kensington Palace. Outnumbered and outgunned, Victoria might well have lost the battle but for the wily Louise Lehzen, who seems to have disliked Conroy even more than Victoria did.

Entering royal service in 1819, the same year as Victoria's birth, Lehzen always quietly took the princess's side against Conroy. After his dismissal when the princess became queen, Lehzen continued to be Victoria's closest friend and confidante – until the arrival of Prince Albert. Like Conroy, Albert disliked and distrusted Lehzen, but there was also an element of jealousy – he did not want a competitor for his wife's affections. Albert's influence was such that, against Victoria's wishes, Lehzen was sent back to Germany.

A key difference between Conroy's desire to control and Lehzen's was the fact that Victoria – as she said herself – 'adored [Lehzen], though I also feared her'. With Conroy there was only fear. Lehzen had the skill to be kind and understanding. Conroy had none of her diplomatic abilities.

It is difficult at this distance in time to judge the precise nature of Victoria's relationship with Conroy. Before she became queen, she and her mother dined regularly with Conroy and his wife, and references in the early journals seem suspiciously neutral in tone; they give no real clue as to her feelings, though we must remember that the journals as we have them now were heavily expurgated after Victoria's death.

But records do exist that show how obsessively and minutely Conroy tried to control if not the princess, then at least the household at Kensington – he drew up a complex list of precise rules for Victoria's twenty-five staff, which turned them from a fairly relaxed body of men and women into what must have seemed like a positively regimented military unit.

He controlled their wages, what they wore, how much coal they were allowed to heat their rooms, their sleeping arrangements, their day-to-day duties and, most importantly, how they were to address the duchess, himself and the princess. He insisted on uniforms – the boys in the steward's room had to wear hats and gloves, the coachman had to wear a cocked hat while driving, and the footmen were obliged to wear green coats and black cravats. Because Victoria had enjoyed gossiping with the staff as a child, he made it a sackable offence for a servant ever to enter Victoria's rooms without being expressly asked by the princess or her governess.

What the servants might have made of Conroy's high-handed ways can be glimpsed in the memoirs of Rose Plummer, who recalled what happened when she worked in a grand London house not far from Kensington Palace in the early part of the twentieth century:

The house, which was just north of Hyde Park, was enormous. It was owned by the duke of somewhere or other – I can't recall his name because we were told never to ask questions about any member of the family and never to say anything at all to each other about who the family were or what they did. If we were heard gossiping, we were out. When I first met her, I thought Mrs W, the housekeeper, was the lady of the house she seemed so grand. She always dressed in black – about eight miles of lace and bombazine but very little jewellery.

She worked for the butler who was even more frightening and grand to us girls. Everything Mrs W said started with the line, 'Mr Tread-gold...' She would say, 'Mr Treadgold expects you to be perfectly turned out each day,' or 'Mr Treadgold expects diligence and hard work and no talking.'

Mr Treadgold loved being able to wield power. He would line all the maids up and check us over once a week; he had a book where, according to your status you were allowed four, six or eight or ten lumps of coal an evening in your room in winter. Every time he lined us up he would point out if our caps had not been straight the previous Wednesday or if we had been a minute late coming down from our rooms.

I was to be a maid of all work but there was also a cook, numerous footmen, gardeners, a butler, senior maids and very senior maids, boot boys and so on. But we all had one thing in common. In the eyes of the nobility we were invisible. We were to be ordered about; we were not allowed to talk to the children of the house, not allowed to use the main staircase, and we had to turn our faces to the wall if we happened along a corridor when a member of the family was using the same corridor. I can't say it was fun!

※

Like all members of her class and background, Victoria expected her servants to be completely devoted to her. Boyfriends were not allowed and time off was severely restricted. Anyone who had the temerity to be ill occasionally was dismissed. Victoria's maid Caroline Lyons was sacked because she had been ill and as a result became 'inattentive and neglectful', as Victoria recorded in her journal in 1833. The fact that Caroline was also 'faithful' seems to have counted for nothing.

As the critic Christopher Marot points out, Victoria was supremely narcissistic; everything centred on her and she expected – as indeed did later royals, perhaps especially the late Queen Mother – that her servants should devote their lives to her, and to her children. Marot points out in an unpublished PhD thesis that Victoria was very good at persuading Parliament to award her nine children substantial annual payments, but made not a single mention in her long life of the appalling treatment of working-class children forced to work fourteen or sixteen hours a day in Britain's coalmines. 'If the modern monarch's role was to advise her ministers, she might have been expected to advise that it was not perhaps a great idea to treat children in this way.'

So the domestic atmosphere at Kensington was entirely coloured by Conroy's desire to show that he was in control.

With Conroy trying to gain ever more influence throughout Kensington Palace, and Lehzen and Victoria and some of the senior servants resenting his high-handed ways, the atmosphere became poisonous. The palace split into factions when it looked increasingly certain that Victoria would become queen; the Duchess of Kent, no doubt egged on by Conroy, began to believe she was perfectly entitled to take over more rooms at Kensington without reference to the king – with the results that we have already seen.

❦

We are lucky today that the magnificent King's Gallery at Kensington did not lose its William Kent ceiling in the early 1830s, because although the duchess's plan to split the king's gallery into three rooms did indeed go ahead, she had the good sense not to damage the ceiling, which was left largely intact.

Other changes to the palace to accommodate the duchess's growing sense of her own importance included moving the Chapel to what had been a kitchen; she also helped herself to the Queen's Bedroom, the State Dressing Room and State Bedroom, the Presence Chamber, the Queen's Drawing Room, the Privy Chamber and the King's Drawing Room.

However much the king allowed, the duchess took more, until crisis point was reached and the king exploded in rage. Victoria would have been oblivious, no doubt, to the dozens of workmen altering, building, demolishing and rebuilding all around her. In fact, precise records of the changes made at this time no longer exist, as the authors of *Kensington Palace: Art, Architecture and Society* point out. The duchess seems to have been in such a hurry that it is as if she was determined get the work finished before she was found out! And behind all her actions was the shadowy figure of Sir John Conroy, who was busy making his own alterations at the palace – we know that he even commissioned a covered walkway across Clock Court to the entrance to the duchess's apartments. The ostensible reason was the first of a series of grand balls the duchess had planned, and it was at one of these balls that what might be described as the most fateful moment in Victoria's life occurred: she met Prince Albert.

✻

Sir John Conroy is perhaps the supreme exemplar of the old adage that pride goeth before a fall. Alterations to the palace, power games played out with the Duchess of Kent, Princess Sophia, Victoria and the staff at Kensington – none of these gave a clue as to how suddenly Conroy would find himself ousted from his life at the very centre of power.

Things actually came to a head many miles from Kensington – at the Albion Hotel at Ramsgate, in fact. Ramsgate was a seaside resort popular with the aristocracy in the 1830s. Almost as soon as Victoria arrived in the summer of 1835, with her mother and numerous servants, she fell ill. No one knows what was wrong with her, but her flu-like symptoms worsened until she seemed very ill indeed. With astonishing tactlessness, and like a vulture spotting a weakness that could be exploited, Conroy apparently entered Victoria's bedroom and tried to persuade her – while she lay propped up by pillows and barely able to think – to give him an absolute assurance that when the king died (he was already very ill by this time), her mother would be made regent and that his position as her most senior adviser would be guaranteed.

Conroy was not so much overly persuasive as bullying. But his tactics failed spectacularly; the young girl he thought would be easy to manipulate resolutely refused. Indeed, Victoria declined to give him any guarantees about anything. It was no doubt at this moment that she determined to get rid of him at the earliest opportunity, which is exactly what she did.

No sooner had she become queen than Conroy, as we have seen, was dismissed without a word. From then on, she seems to have done everything possible to avoid meeting him. Victoria's mother was allowed to remain at Kensington Palace, but Victoria moved immediately to Buckingham Palace, never to return to the scenes of her troubled childhood. Conroy spent the rest of his life complaining to anyone who would listen that he had been treated abominably.

CHAPTER ELEVEN

MARRIAGE À LA MODE

*'Both Edward VII and George VI were really called Albert, but the royal
family wouldn't let them use the name on the throne out of reverence
for Queen Victoria's Consort, and the Privy Council wouldn't allow it
either, because the name Albert sounded so common.'*

KYRIL BONFIGLIOLI

I f Kensington had been an aunt (and uncle) heap when Princess
Victoria lived there, it became ever more so after her departure.
She was proclaimed queen at St James's Palace on 21 June 1837 and
left Kensington Palace finally and for ever on 13 July. From that point
on, royal hangers-on, eccentric retired equerries, widowed cousins,
nephews and nieces of various royal relatives and of course numerous
aunts and uncles lived in the decaying muddle that Kensington Palace
gradually became.

The queen's mother, never entirely forgiven for not protecting her
daughter from the monstrous Sir John Conroy, was forced to accept

that she would no longer have access to her daughter at Buckingham Palace. The duchess, who never learned to speak English well, was to stay on at Kensington until her death in 1861, by which time Victoria had softened to her memory. After the duchess's death, Princess Mary and her husband the Duke of Teck came to live at the palace. Their daughter Victoria Mary – known as Mary from 1923 – was born in 1867 at the palace, and so we peek a little into the early twentieth century, but just for a moment.

Back in 1819 when Victoria left for good, the palace ceased to be central to the life of the royal family. Writing in 1923, Ernest Law summarises what happened between the accession of Queen Victoria and the restoration of the palace in 1898:

> During all those years, the palace had been suffered gradually more and more to fall into a deplorable state of disrepair. The walls were … shored up; the rafters of the roof were beginning to rot away, tiles and slates were broken and slipping off the roof so that it was becoming increasingly difficult to keep the wind and rain at bay. The floors were everywhere deteriorating, the panelled walls and ceilings of the great reception rooms slowly but surely crumbling to decay.

Victoria's love for Kensington Palace – a love that prompted her to save it from certain destruction towards the end of her reign – cannot have anything to do with the darker aspects of her early life there; aspects summed up when, years after she had left for Buckingham Palace, her half-sister Princess Feodore wrote to her saying, 'I escaped some years of imprisonment [at Kensington Palace] which you, my poor dear sister had to endure, after I was married.' No, it seems it was not even her close relationship with Feodore that compelled Victoria to save her childhood home. The real reason, perhaps, was that, aged seventeen in 1836, it was at Kensington that Princess Victoria met the first of the two great loves of her life: Albert, the man who was to become her husband. She may have screamed and hurled things at him throughout their marriage; she may have considered him her social inferior; but he could well have been the first man to show a physical interest in a young woman whose early years had been all about repression. For that, she could (and did) forgive him everything. And it was the memory of him rather than the reality that she really loved. When he was no longer there to argue and sulk about his lack of power, she remembered only his early passion and so she virtually beatified him – every aspect of their lives together became part of the hallowed myth she created: one that made Albert a saint and his children a permanent disappointment to Victoria because they did not live up to 'dear Albert's' high ideals.

And if all this was true (and few historians have denied it) then no one was going to be allowed to destroy the very place – the hallowed ground, as it were – where she and Albert first met.

❧

Victoria had so many German and Dutch relations that she might easily have married someone other than Albert, especially as King William IV (no doubt partly to show the Duchess of Kent who was really in charge) had decided that Victoria should marry into the House of

Orange. Prince Alexander of the Netherlands, the second son of the Prince of Orange, he insisted, was the obvious choice.

Alexander and his elder brother were invited to London in 1836, but at precisely the same time the Duchess of Kent, egged on by Conroy and her brother Leopold, invited Victoria's Coburg cousins Ernest and Albert to London. William IV was furious but then almost everything the duchess did in relation to Victoria (and Kensington Palace) infuriated him. He approached the government in an attempt to prevent Albert and Ernest coming to London. The attempt failed because the government refused to intervene. Foreign Secretary Lord Palmerston advised the king that what he was proposing would make him look ridiculous.

Alexander and his brother duly arrived and the king laid on lavish entertainments for them at Windsor. Unfortunately, Victoria found them deathly dull. But delighted as she must have been at this development, the duchess's plans did not work out quite as she had hoped. Her idea had been to marry Victoria to Ernest not Albert.

Victoria may have had a sixth sense that Albert was likely to prove the better husband – certainly, Ernest demonstrated in later life that he was far more like the 'wicked uncles' than Albert. Both he and the woman he eventually married, Princess Alexandrine of Baden, were extremely promiscuous. They were also very unhappy and eventually divorced. Conversely, Albert proved to be similar to George III in his desire for a strict, moral family life with not a mistress in sight.

Indeed, Albert appears to have been strict to the point of puritanism from his earliest days – and he shared this trait with Victoria. The princess also apparently thought him very beautiful when she first saw him, in 1836, apparently on the great staircase at Kensington Palace, but she cannot have imagined that she would eventually have nine children with him, all of whom went on to marry into major European royal families.

Albert stayed at Kensington for several weeks during that first visit and Victoria confided to her diary that he and his brother Ernest were 'natural' and kind. She wrote: 'The more I see of them ... the more I love them.'

By 1839 Victoria had met Albert again and spent a great deal more time with him. They probably reached some kind of private understanding – she confided to her diary that Albert had at one point written to say, 'I love you so much ... I can't say how much.' Victoria was entranced. She would also have known that her mother and her uncle Leopold, whose judgement she trusted, were keen for the match to go ahead. Victoria wrote to Leopold from Kensington:

My Dearest Uncle,

These few lines will be given to you by my dear uncle Ernest, when he sees you.

I must thank you, my beloved Uncle, for the prospect of great happiness you have contributed to give me, in the person of dear Albert. Allow me, then, my dearest Uncle, to tell you how delighted I am with him, and how much I like him in every way. He possesses every quality that could be desired to render me perfectly happy. He is so sensible, so kind, and so good, and so amiable too. He has, besides, the most pleasing and delightful exterior and appearance you can possibly see.

I have only now to beg you, my dearest Uncle, to take care of the health of one, now so dear to me, and to take him under your special protection. I hope and trust that all will go on prosperously and well, on this subject of so much importance to me.

Believe me always, my dearest uncle, your most affectionate devoted and grateful niece,

Victoria

Victoria proposed to Albert at Windsor, where, because she was now queen, she had to ask for his hand rather than the other way around. It was one of those unavoidable anomalies that occurs if you allow women to become queen, and the fact that this was a rare but necessary disruption of the nineteenth-century insistence on men being in charge in all things cannot have made it easy for Albert. In fact, it was the start of a resentment about his position as Victoria's inferior that was to last for the rest of his life. At Windsor on 15 October 1839 she confided to her diary that she had sent for Albert, sat him down on a sofa and told him that 'it would make me too happy if he would consent to what I wanted (that he should marry me). We embraced each other over and over again and he was so affectionate.'

By now Victoria's childhood at Kensington Palace was already receding in her memory. Such momentous things had happened since she became queen that her dislike of the Kensington System and all that it had done to her was already beginning to soften. In her journal for 13 July 1837, her first day of freedom from her mother, Conroy and their suffocating rules, she had written:

Got up at 8. At half past nine we breakfasted. It was the last time that

I slept in this poor old palace, as I go to Buckingham Palace today. Though I rejoice to go into Buckingham Palace for many reasons, it is not without feelings of regret that I shall bid adieu forever (that is, forever as a dwelling) to this my birthplace, where I have been born and bred, and to which I am really attached! I have seen my dear sister married here, I have seen many of my dear relations here, I have had pleasant balls and delicious concerts here, my present rooms upstairs are really very pleasant, comfortable and pretty and enfin I like this poor palace. I have held my first council here too!

And then perhaps thinking of Conroy she continues, 'I have gone through painful and disagreeable scenes here, 'tis true, but still I am fond of this poor old palace.'

Long before Victoria abandoned Kensington Palace for Buckingham Palace – a move designed, in part at least, to draw a line between Victoria the put-upon princess and Victoria the formidable queen – Kensington had become a home for minor royals. Indeed, Victoria had only ever been a minor royal herself until changing circumstances and a host of misbehaving uncles meant that she suddenly found herself a very important royal indeed.

But while Victoria was suffering under the Kensington System, which gave her no peace and no privacy, other distant royals were squirrelled away in other parts of the palace, and despite Victoria's mother's insistence that more and more space should be given over to her use as Victoria's chances of becoming queen increased, there was still plenty of room for other royals and their teams of servants.

If we are tempted to think of Kensington Palace as a moderate-sized country house – and many people have insisted that that is all it is – let us not forget that, to gain some idea of its real size, Kensington Palace had almost 250 working chimneys in its heyday, not to mention miles of passageways and hidden staircases (for the servants), all built behind endless grand rooms, privies and servants' rooms; many of these were altered, partitioned, extended and rebuilt over the generations and centuries so that Kensington became a veritable warren.

Rather than referring to Kensington as the 'aunt heap' – as Edward VII famously labelled it in the mid-twentieth century – we should perhaps more accurately think of the old palace, at least with regard to its inhabitants towards the end of the eighteenth century, as an 'uncle heap', for it was George III who looked eagerly towards Kensington as a home for his many sons (nine in all, of whom seven survived into adulthood).

In fact, had it not been for George III's need to house his numerous offspring, Kensington Palace would almost certainly have been sold or demolished. After George II's death, the palace had become rather like Miss Havisham's house – it was left cobwebbed, abandoned and unloved by George III, with only a few old retainers kept in situ simply to keep an eye on things, and to raise the alarm only if the walls and ceilings seemed quite literally on the verge of collapse. Various apartments were locked up and inspected only occasionally; the great state rooms grew damp and gathered thick layers of dust, for this was long before anyone would have thought of an old house as a national treasure or something to be preserved for historical reasons.

And as the eighteenth century wore on, the monarch's new role as head of state – a role that, as we will recall, meant governing rather than ruling – attracted additional scrutiny and subsequent criticism when the royal family seemed to be misbehaving or spending too much money. Until the last of the Stuart kings was exiled, the monarch could do as he or she pleased, and Parliament rarely put its foot down. In George III's time, by contrast, Parliament was increasingly concerned with making sure the royal family's finances were at least kept under control. In the distant past, Kensington, like the other royal palaces, would have been maintained simply because it was one of the royal residences; now people began to question whether the king really needed an old palace he no longer used. How could the cost to the public be justified?

It is doubtful that George III (in his sane moments) had any senti-mental idea that Kensington Palace should be preserved for its own sake, but as his sons reached adulthood in the 1790s he determined that he would deflect any criticism of his financial affairs by pointing to his economical reuse of an old palace to house his sons. None of this was of any relevance to his daughters, of course, as they would simply be married off to princes with palaces of their own.

We have seen how Victoria's father, the Duke of Kent, came to live at Kensington, but several of George III's other sons also took the country road to the palace, including the man who was later to become Queen Victoria's favourite uncle: Augustus, Duke of Sussex. Augustus was the ninth child and sixth son of George III and like several of his brothers he rebelled against his overly moralistic, censorious upbringing.

Born in 1773 at Buckingham House (as Buckingham Palace was

then known), he was whisked across the road to St James's Palace to be baptised, and from then on, he was kept carefully at home, where he was taught by a succession of tutors but given little freedom. Indeed, it was in the year preceding Augustus's birth that his father, increasingly obsessed with controlling his children's lives, persuaded Parliament to pass the Royal Marriages Act, which enshrined in law a key element of George's regime of control. The Act made any marriage by a member of the royal family invalid unless the marriage had first been agreed by the monarch. It was this same Act that, two centuries later, helped to ruin Princess Margaret's chance of happiness – Queen Elizabeth II was persuaded by her advisers (especially Tommy Lascelles) to tell Margaret that if she married without the monarch's permission, the marriage would be invalid. Indeed, Margaret was told in no uncertain terms that without that permission she would be unable to find a churchman in England who would agree to conduct the marriage. Her only option would be to leave the country, marry in a civil ceremony and more than likely lose all her royal privileges. It never seems to have occurred to anyone that, just as the original law was instituted at the insistence of a mad monarch, it might be repealed by a sane one.

Sanity was not a strong point among the Hanoverian kings. For George III, control was key and he must have assumed that even if his sons objected to him having a potential veto over any woman they might want to marry, they would accept it rather than lose the chance to become king (or at least sire heirs to the throne).

In this he failed miserably to understand just how rebellious his actions were likely to make his sons. The most rebellious in terms of mistresses and illegitimate offspring, as we have seen, was the Duke of

Clarence (later William IV), who had ten children with his long-term mistress, but the other brothers all took mistresses or married without permission or both.

The Duke of Kent agreed to drop his mistress for money and for the chance to sire an heir, but none of this bothered the delightfully eccentric Duke of Sussex, who became a lifelong resident of Kensington Palace.

Very early on, while still a teenager, he had refused a career in the military, which was the traditional and expected career path of Hanoverian sons. His brothers seem to have slightly despised him for this; the Duke of Kent insisted, 'I have been educated in the field, my brother in the closet.' Of course, the Duke of Kent failed to see the irony in this – he may have been a soldier, but it will be recalled that he was a very bad one.

As with the Duke of Kent, the Duke of Sussex was given his large apartment at Kensington long before he actually moved in. During his long years at Kensington, Augustus earned a name for himself as an unusual character, but his reputation had been forming long before this. It was a reputation based on the fact that he stood in opposition to almost everything for which his father and his brothers stood. He was considered as mad as his father by many during his lifetime, but today his 'mad' views and opinions seem remarkably liberal and humane.

The dominating fact of Augustus Frederick's life was that, unlike his brothers, he suffered very badly from asthma. He was also unlike most of his brothers in that he was immensely tall – well over six feet, in fact, which was unusual for the time.

At the age of just fourteen he had been sent to the University of

Göttingen in Germany, but he seems to have spent most of the next few years going to parties rather than doing any work. Socially confident, he was distinguished only by his vanity. According to Roger Fulford, writing early in the 1920s, Augustus met a woman at dinner who, on hearing him sing, complimented him on his voice. She was astonished to hear the following reply: 'I have the most wonderful voice that ever was heard – three octaves – and I do understand music.'

During the winter of 1792, when he was nineteen, Augustus set off for Rome, which was then a magnet for the young and wealthy in search of fun. Rome had the sort of reputation that Paris had in the 1920s – exciting, slightly dangerous and with an undercurrent of sexual licence. Augustus no doubt persuaded his father to allow him to winter in the city on the grounds that it would be good for his asthma, but Augustus seems to have made full use of his time there to chase women.

He also – no doubt to the fury of his brother the Prince of Wales – paid a visit to a man who many in Britain felt should, by rights, have been king. This was a third cousin twice removed of George III; he styled himself as Henry IX, the last legitimate descendant of James II. He was also known as the Cardinal Duke of York or the Cardinal of York. He was rich, a notable eccentric and behaved in a grand manner that suggested he really thought he might be summoned back to England at any moment to assume the throne.

Augustus's great offence was to call on the Cardinal Duke, bow before him and insist on addressing him as 'Your Royal Highness'. The Cardinal Duke was so delighted that the two men began to exchange visits. It is easy to imagine how much Augustus would have enjoyed knowing that when news of these visits reached England, his brother the Prince of Wales would be incensed.

Augustus's other great offence was not that he chased women in Rome; that was almost considered a requirement for any self-respecting aristocratic Englishman enjoying the Grand Tour. No, Augustus made the mistake – if it can be called a mistake – of falling in love. The object of his attentions was Lady Augusta Murray, who was visiting the city with her mother and sister.

The story goes that Augustus met Lady Augusta on the steps of the church of San Giacomo on the Via del Corso. Noticing that Lady Augusta's shoe had come undone, Augustus knelt to retie it and struck up a conversation.

Perhaps inevitably for a man who was later to amass a vast collection of books at Kensington, Augustus seems to have tried to woo Lady Augusta via the printed word. He sent her a copy of *The Tempest*, for example, and heavily underlined the following:

> O if a virgin and your affections not gone forth,
> I'll make you the Queen of Naples.

Augustus was trading on his royal status, but he could no more make Augusta Queen of Naples than he could make her Queen of England; no doubt the sentiment appealed to his literary tastes and to his sense of his own importance. Certainly, the literary approach seems to have persuaded Augusta, who welcomed regular visits from the young man from then on, as indeed did her mother.

Augustus became obsessed. When he wasn't visiting Augusta for tea or meeting her at various evening parties around the city, he wrote passionate if eccentric love letters, bestowing an immediate nickname upon the object of his affections. He addressed her as 'my amiable Goosy'. In one letter he wrote, 'Ye Gods, my Gussy, how well you looked last night!'

Lady Augusta seems to have been dazzled by her young admirer – Augustus was six years her junior – and readily accepted his proposal of marriage. Even as he proposed, Augustus would have known that the marriage would be likely to be declared invalid under the provisions of his father's Royal Marriages Act. But by now Augustus was so smitten that he would have said and promised almost anything to get Augusta into bed.

This was, in a sense, the beginning of a lifetime of Augustus doing and saying things with which his brothers heartily disagreed. He was above all things a contrarian – perhaps even a genuine revolutionary.

Augustus's plan reached its apogee when he committed himself to marriage by writing to Augusta – a written promise of marriage at this time had the force of law (although arguably this may not have applied to members of the royal family) and it was not uncommon for young men to be sued for breach of promise if they reneged on such a vow. Augustus's proposal could hardly have been more fulsome:

On my knees before God our creator, I Augustus Frederick promise thee Augusta Murray and swear upon the Bible, as I hope for salvation in the world to come, that I will take thee Augusta Murray for my wife: for richer or for poorer: in sickness and in health: to love and to cherish until death us do part: to love but thee only and none other: and may

God forget me if I forget thee. The Lord's name be praised! So bless me! Oh God! And with my hand writing do I Augustus Frederick this sign March 21, 1793 at Rome and put my seal to it and my name.

By this time Lady Augusta had clearly agreed to the marriage, but she knew that, not being a Catholic, she could not be married by a priest in a Catholic church, so she and Augustus cast about to find someone else to conduct the marriage. Eventually Augustus tracked down an English clergyman who was visiting Rome and who agreed to officiate. Augustus, fearing that Augusta might demur even at this late stage, wrote: 'If Gunn [the clergyman] will not marry us, I will die...'

Soon after this, the couple agreed to meet the Reverend Gunn one evening at Augusta's hotel while her mother, Lady Dunmore, was absent at a party. Without a single witness the marriage ceremony was completed. The couple initially told no one, which meant that for the next few weeks the abnormally tall Augustus had to climb a drainpipe late each night and squeeze in through a window to be with his new wife.

At some point that summer, Lady Augusta's mother decided it was time to move on to Florence, which they duly did. Augustus followed them and no doubt continued his clandestine visits to his new wife – they had to be clandestine as Augusta's mother still had no idea her daughter was married. Indeed, the prince told his mother-in-law only when it became obvious that Lady Augusta was pregnant. We don't know how Lady Dunmore reacted, but any disapproval must have been tempered by the fact that Augustus, though clearly eccentric, was a prince. Knowing her daughter was pregnant, Lady Dunmore set off for England with her, but by this time news of Augustus's relationship, if not marriage, had reached the court in England and he was ordered to return. By the time Augustus reached London, Lady Augusta and her mother were living on Lower Berkeley Street in Mayfair. At least now Augustus could visit his wife via the front door.

It is highly likely that, given the nature of their hotel wedding, Augustus would have promised his new wife that they would be married in a more formal manner on their return to England; a manner likely to be more acceptable to the court. And so it was that they were quietly married at St George's Hanover Square in December 1793.

The inevitable storm broke in January 1794 when, Augusta having given birth to a boy, who was christened Augustus Frederick like his father, the king became fully aware of what was going on. Augustus was told to leave the country while the king ordered the Court of Arches, an ecclesiastical court which at that time decided on divorces, to annul the marriage on the grounds that the king's permission had not been obtained.

Suddenly, Augusta found herself unmarried. Still in thrall to his passion, Augustus somehow arranged fake documentation for his wife and she was able to leave the country despite the king having forbidden it. The couple met again in Berlin and lived there as man and wife for several years while the king fumed in London. Their second child was born in Germany.

Clearly in some financial difficulty, Augustus returned to London in 1800. He was now twenty-seven and convinced Parliament would grant him an independent allowance. In fact, the grant was refused. Finding himself with no income must have been a shock, but from the king's point of view it had the desired effect. In 1801 Augustus agreed to have nothing more to do with Augusta in return for a dukedom (he became

Duke of Sussex) and a grant of £12,000 a year. Of this he gave one third to Augusta and her two children, but it seems he never saw her again.

By 1806 his former passion had turned to anger, and he took Augusta to court for calling herself the Duchess of Sussex. In 1809 he was back in court, where an order was made that the children should live with him. One wonders if the court gave Augusta a fair hearing; the perceived importance of a royal duke almost certainly swayed the court in favour of the petitioner.

The Duke of Sussex's life through these years gives no real indication of what he was to become. Indeed, his adventures in Italy and prosecution of his own wife suggest he was just another 'wicked uncle'. But Augustus's liberal sympathies, at least in the political arena, were genuine. His brothers were all violently Tory as they grew older, despite their claims to be liberal Whigs.

The Duke of Sussex, on the other hand, was the real thing. No sooner had he received his grant and divested himself of his wife than he settled into his spacious apartment at Kensington Palace and began his career as a subversive. He moved his collection of Bibles and other early books into the palace and began the mania for collecting that never left him. His attitude and opinions may have alienated him from the royal family, but they made him hugely popular with the public.

By 1810 his passion for collecting had led to massive debts and a correspondingly massive increase in the number of books and manuscripts he kept at Kensington. No doubt the old floors groaned under the weight of the bookcases he had installed along virtually every wall. Many of these beautifully made bookcases survived until the 1960s when, as with so much of the early contents of the palace, they were unceremoniously removed and destroyed.

A particular passion of the duke's seems to have been biblical history, and his studies led to his decision – one that deeply shocked his family – to support moves towards Catholic emancipation. This seemed an especially terrible betrayal to his brothers since Hanoverian legitimacy rested on the premise that Catholicism, with its links to Stuart absolutism, should not be tolerated.

But the Duke of Sussex embraced the cause wholeheartedly. He spoke at great length on numerous occasions in favour of emancipation in the House of Lords between 1810 and 1829 and seemed at times to have been determined to wear the opposition down by the sheer duration of his speeches.

On one occasion he had spoken for so long that a Tory peer whispered to his neighbour, 'His Royal Highness is deep in the Councils of Trent.' To which his neighbour replied, 'I could wish it was the river Trent.'

But if the duke's promotion of Catholic emancipation upset the royal family, it was as nothing to his support for his niece Princess Charlotte, daughter of the duke's brother the Prince of Wales. The prince had publicly fallen out with his daughter when she refused to marry a dull Dutch prince he had chosen for her. After the Prince of Wales berated her, Charlotte had run away to her mother's house. The Duke of York, along with a number of Whig politicians, advised her to return to Carlton House, where she lived with her father. The prince, still furious, had her sent to Cranbourne House in Windsor, from where she sent her uncle, the Duke of Sussex a (presumably plaintive) letter. When he heard she was being held a virtual prisoner there, he threatened to expose his brother by speaking on the subject in the House of Lords. Soon after, he made good on his threat. His fellow peers were deeply embarrassed that royal linen was being washed in public, so to speak, but Augustus's speech seems to have had the desired effect – Charlotte was allowed enough freedom at least to ride in the park.

The Prince Regent never forgave his brother for this public humiliation, but Augustus refused to apologise and indeed he seems to have cared nothing for his brother's views on this or any other matter.

It was almost as if a spirit of devilment ran parallel with Augustus's sense of his own importance. In 1820, by which time the Regent had become George IV, Augustus committed the ultimate sin so far as his brother was concerned: he befriended Caroline of Brunswick, the Princess of Wales (now queen), whom his brother had tried so long to divorce. Augustus was no fool and he knew that Caroline was immensely popular, if for no other reason than that her husband was widely disliked. Augustus made a widely publicised visit to Caroline and, almost overnight, he became one of the most popular men in the country. He continued to visit and support her until her death in 1821.

It was only ten years later when George IV was dying that some form of reconciliation took place between the two brothers – eccentrically enough, the practical side of the effort to make up for past quarrels came initially from Augustus. Hearing that his brother was stuck in bed, Augustus told his servants to put his asthma chair on a cart and have it driven to his dying brother at Windsor. The enormous chair

– specially made so that the asthmatic Augustus could sleep sitting up – would have made the king's last few days more bearable.

After George's death, Augustus became ever more radical – he laid the foundation stone for London University, a university designed to get round the fact that dissenters could not take the oath of allegiance and therefore could not study at Oxford or Cambridge, the two primary English institutions for higher education at the time. Now dissenters had a university of their own.

When William IV came to the throne following the death of George IV, Augustus was made Ranger of Hyde Park and St James's Park, and his parliamentary grant increased to £18,000 a year. Now he threw his weight behind the Great Reform Bill, which was passed by the Commons in 1831 and rejected by a House of Lords stuffed with diehard Tory peers. The Bill had been designed to put an end to various corrupt parliamentary practices, chief among them the fact that in many areas up to a dozen boroughs, each electing an individual MP, might be under the control of a single landowner.

When the House of Lords rejected the Bill, peers no doubt thought that would be the end of the matter; but they had reckoned without the Duke of Sussex. Although Earl Grey was the driving force behind the Reform Bill, Augustus had his own part in its success, lobbying his brother William IV to create enough new peers to ensure the Reform Bill was passed. William was furious and told Augustus he never wanted to see him again. But public pressure was mounting and at last the Reform Bill was passed. Augustus became something of a hero.

He seems genuinely to have felt that the poorer sections of society should be involved in making decisions about how the country was run. Or perhaps he simply enjoyed annoying his brother.

The Duke of Sussex's estranged wife Lady Augusta lived on until 1830. The duke himself lived until 1843 and became increasingly reclusive in his final years. He spent less time away from Kensington Palace, where his idiosyncrasies grew ever more noticeable. Many of these arose from his sense of his own permanent ill-health, especially his asthma. He became increasingly hypochondriac. Everywhere in his extensive apartment, piles of books grew taller and on the piles were to be found an ever-increasing number of bottles of patent medicines. Day and night, Augustus – who found it almost impossible to sleep for long because of his asthma – would wander the corridors and gardens at Kensington wearing a large black skull cap and a long gown. He refused ever to remove the cap on the grounds that he had done so once – for a group portrait of his niece Victoria's accession – only to fall ill with a severe cold that brought on his asthma. After that he never removed it again.

His health obsessions had other odd consequences – from his vast collection of medicine bottles he once happened to pick up a bottle of liniment and, his sight by now being rather poor, he assumed it was designed to be swallowed. He drank the whole bottle and was violently sick.

By 1832 he was suffering from cataracts and he made the courageous decision to have what was then a dangerous operation to remove them. The operation was successful, his eyesight improved and he celebrated by accepting an offer to became president of the Royal Society.

As he aged, his compulsion to buy books and manuscripts he could not afford grew worse. He petitioned Parliament for more money, but it was clear that his living expenses were now minimal – he just wanted the money in order to add even more to his vast collection of books, stuffed animals, minerals, rocks and other curiosities.

The Times mocked him in verse for his perpetual demands for more money:

> A friend to the Whigs I have been and shall be
> O liberals, wherefore so stingy to me?
> Ye envy not Daniel O'Connell his rent:
> Ye paid off the debts of the Duchess of Kent!
> And then let me go, with a dog and a string
> To beg through the land – like the son of a king.
> Pity the sorrows of a poor old duke
> Whose trembling limbs have brought him to your door
> With twenty thousand on his banker's book,
> He asks, for science sake, a little more.

But if he failed to get as much money as he wanted, he did at least get a new wife following the death of Lady Augusta. He married (again without royal permission) the delightfully named widow Lady Cecilia Buggin in 1831. She was nearly two decades younger than Augustus and had been his mistress for some years prior to the marriage, which took place at St George's Hanover Square, where, of course, Augustus had married his first wife nearly forty years earlier. He must have known that once again his marriage was legally invalid, because he had not obtained permission from his brother William IV, but in his typical rebellious way he went ahead with it anyway. But poor Cecilia was not allowed to style herself Duchess of Sussex and instead reverted to her maiden name, Underwood.

Queen Victoria, who adored the Duke of Sussex, made Lady Cecilia Duchess of Inverness in her own right in 1840 and what had been a marriage without royal permission became, almost by stealth, a marriage accepted and condoned by the highest in the land. Queen Victoria even invited Cecilia to dinner, although she was allowed to join the monarch's table only after all the other duchesses had sat down. It wasn't a snub but merely a recognition that the Duchess of Inverness had only recently been ennobled; all the other women had older titles.

By the time he died in 1843, Augustus's library at Kensington included more than 5,000 Bibles. Many were unique examples. His library – which gradually took over much of his Kensington Palace apartment – was divided into sections. The Bibles were kept in what he liked to call the Divinity Room.

He had long cultivated his own garden at Kensington – he gardened for colour, he said, and every spring and summer his blooms were widely admired. Unlike his brother the Duke of Kent, who was never happy with his apartment, Augustus was delighted with what he had been given and spent money only on miles of shelves for his books.

For the last decade of his life, his rooms at Kensington – including his much-loved library – were all kept with their interconnecting doors permanently open so that his collection of songbirds could be released from their cages to fly about as they pleased, the duke always being careful to first ask a servant to ensure all the external windows were closed.

His favourite personal servant was a diminutive black boy the duke insisted on calling Mr Blackman, and he employed another servant whose time was almost entirely devoted to winding and adjusting the duke's vast collection of clocks. The result was that on the hour (and in many cases on the half-hour and quarter-hour) his apartment was filled with bells and gongs striking, musical tunes, national anthems and martial airs. The noise must have been deafening, but the duke absolutely refused to have any clock turned off.

His passion for clocks extended also to watches – he kept eighteen in a glass case and, like the clocks, they had to be wound every day.

But despite the duke's increasing eccentricity he did not become entirely reclusive. He was a son of George III with no prospect of becoming king, but he was a celebrity of sorts and as a member of the royal family he inevitably attracted attention; perhaps his visitors hoped that despite his distance from the crown he might have some influence and so they called on him in the mornings. He greeted them in his sitting room dressed in an extraordinary violet satin gown that reached to the ground. Under this he wore a white silk waistcoat and, on his head, of course, that perpetual black silk cap.

The fact that he saw his visitors in the morning was an echo of the court levee and, once it was over, he retreated to his library to read. If a passage interested him particularly, he would draw a small black ink hand with an extended finger pointing to the relevant section. Many of his books ended up in the British Library, where the little black hands can still be seen in the margins of the books he once owned.

He also wrote little comments: 'A most mischievous argument' appears in his copy of Gladstone's *Church and State*, along with 'This is merely declamatory – no argument.' In keeping with a lifetime of revolutionary thought, there is a comment in one of his prayer books that shocked the elderly bibliophile who bought the prayer book after the duke's death. Augustus had written in the margin against the statement of the Athanasian Creed: 'I don't believe a word of it.' It seems that in private he was even more radical than he had been in public.

Although he lived to a good age by the standards of the late eighteenth and early nineteenth centuries, his health was probably not improved by an addiction in the last years of his life to turtle soup and ice cream. He apparently ate almost nothing else. He died on 21 April 1843, and in one of a series of final acts of defiance, insisted that he be buried not in the royal cemetery at Windsor but in the public cemetery at Kensal Green. This was deeply shocking to a society that was obsessed with proprieties – a royal prince should not be buried among commoners – but since Augustus had insisted, it was felt that his wishes must be carried out.

Perhaps even more shockingly, it was discovered that the duke had insisted his body be 'opened up' after his death. Most Britons were still believers, if not devout Christians, in this pre-Darwinian era, and the facts of the resurrection – including the idea that one would get one's body back – meant there was a huge prejudice against leaving one's body to science. The Duke of Sussex thought this was all nonsense and welcomed the fact that his corpse might do some good. In his will he wrote: 'In quitting this state of existence, it may be some

consolation to feel that, even after death, my bodily frame may advance
that which I always desired in my life – the good of my fellow men.'

Augustus's apartment at Kensington, offered to him in 1805, had formerly been the housekeeper's apartment. It overlooked Clock Court
and seems to have been too small – probably only because the duke
needed space for his growing collection of books and curios. Unlike
many residents, he seems to have been successful in taking over more
space than he was originally granted without causing a huge row!

'By 1810,' according to the official history of the palace, edited by
Olivia Fryman, 'most of the old courtiers' range extending around the
Stone Gallery to the west of the state apartments had been offered to
him.'

As we have seen, he was not as fussy about his various residences
as some of his brothers and he seems to have been reasonably happy
not to employ numerous teams of architects and designers to turn his
apartment into something grand and imposing. But the pressure of all
those books began to tell, and during the 1830s he was forced to add
library after library until there were six in total, each devoted to one
or other of his interests – in addition to the Bibles, there were books
of military history and books by ancient Greek and Latin authors; he
even had a Masonic library, and created a Masonic Lodge, where he
would regularly meet his fellow masons.

Towards the end of his life the duke's passion for collecting became
almost pathological. His collection of cigars, for example, was enormous and, when sold after his death, raised more money than all his

silver put together; he had also expanded his collection of rare early religious manuscripts and at his death these numbered more than 12,000. But as we saw from his contemptuous note about the Athanasian Creed, Augustus clearly found it impossible to accept the supernatural elements of religion – his interest seems to have been more academic than spiritual, which may explain why his collection included rare Jewish texts and even an early copy of the Quran.

His bedroom at the palace seems to have been relatively modest, but we know that he paid for the finest scarlet silk to line his bookshelves; crimson damask was installed at great expense across the fronts of his bookshelves to keep out the dust, and wooden shutters were added to the windows to stop the sunlight fading the spines of the books. The duke had even had gas lights installed, no doubt so that he could read more easily late into the night.

He had hoped that his whole collection might go the British Museum (which then housed the British Library), but it was not to be, and his vast collection was dispersed after his death in 1843.

CHAPTER TWELVE

A NEST OF GENTLEFOLK

'An ugly baby is a very nasty object – and the prettiest is frightful.'
QUEEN VICTORIA

Everyone who writes about Kensington Palace seems convinced that no sooner had one resident died or moved elsewhere than their apartments were desperately in need of complete renovation and modernisation – one might even think that no sooner had residents of the great palace arrived than they began wrecking the place in their individual ways. Where other houses might become dusty and dirty and perhaps even unfashionable over the years, Kensington Palace – if we are to believe many commentators – is always in need of major work. What was acceptable accommodation for one generation becomes completely intolerable for the next generation.

What is probably meant is that the layout and decorative elements of apartments that were acceptable to the Duke of Sussex or the Duke of Kent quickly came to seem old-fashioned, and new generations of junior royals could hardly be expected to live in dated apartments.

Thus it has often been the case that with the notable exception of the state apartments, Kensington Palace has suffered an almost endless series of modernisations, including many that were later regretted as they involved tearing down important (and sometimes very beautiful) early parts of the building in order to install modern conveniences that were bound, in their turn, to be ripped out.

After the Duke of Sussex died in 1843, only his widow survived from a generation that had included the numerous sons and daughters of George III. The bird-like Duchess of Inverness, now a respectable widow whose early moral turpitude as the Duke of Sussex's second illegitimate bride was long forgotten, lived on at Kensington until as late as 1873, but her fellow residents changed and she was joined by more distant members of the royal family whose lives at the palace were to extend well into the twentieth century.

Kensington Palace in the second half of the nineteenth century is perhaps most associated with the relatives of Queen Victoria, especially her children and grandchildren, but there were also cousins, and there is no doubt Victoria enjoyed being able to reward relatives she liked with apartments at the palace.

She was able to do this because of a clever pact she made with the government. She agreed to open the state apartments to the public, knowing that this would forestall complaints about the cost of repairing and modernising the palace.

She issued the following announcement:

Her Majesty, in her desire to gratify the wishes of her people, has directed that the state rooms at Kensington Palace, in the central part of the building, which has been closed and unoccupied since 1760, together with Sir Christopher Wren's Banqueting Room, attached to the palace, shall, after careful restoration be opened to the public.

The public eagerly queued to get a chance to see inside a royal palace, a concept that was entirely new. Meanwhile, the vast bulk of the palace, which was and still is closed to the public, could be modernised for the queen's extensive list of family members in need of a London residence.

The gardens were also increasingly democratised – bathing had been allowed (for men only) in the Serpentine from 1866 and walls and ditches that had cut the palace off from the surrounding park were gradually removed.

Slotting her relatives into her old home gave Victoria an additional dose of something she had always craved: control. Not since George III had a monarch exercised such complete – and sometimes rather cruel – authority over her relatives, and especially her children.

Victoria and Albert's almost brutal treatment of their son and heir, Albert, later Edward VII, is well known, but as her other children grew up (especially her daughters), she was to dominate their lives too.

Before their marriages, Victoria's daughters were expected to work as her secretaries, often for very long hours. One can easily imagine that their enthusiasm to be married might have had something to do with the need to escape their mother – for marriage really was the only means of escape for her female children; careers in any meaningful sense were largely out of the question.

One or two of Victoria's children would certainly have preferred a career outside dynastic marriage, and this is especially true of Princess Louise (1848–1939), who was to live at Kensington Palace for more than half a century, from 1883 until her death aged ninety-one in 1939.

Louise's start in life was bizarre. Her mother had already had five children by the time Louise was born in 1848, and we know from Victoria's journals that she hated pregnancy and childbirth, so it is hard to imagine that this was a particularly welcome addition to the family. At her baptism, the assembled guests were horrified when at the critical moment the elderly Duchess of Gloucester, a daughter of George III, suddenly threw herself at the feet of Victoria with her hands upraised. What on earth was going on? It seems that the duchess had become confused and forgot she was attending a baptism – she thought the ceremony had something to do with kissing the hands of a new monarch. She was hastened to her feet by various attendants and the ceremony continued.

As she grew, Louise developed a talent for art. At a time when virtually every aristocratic girl in England was taught to draw – along with music, art was considered sufficiently ladylike to be encouraged in the daughters of the well-to-do – this may not seem unusual, but Louise seems to have had an exceptional gift. When Lord Tennyson's son Hallam visited Osborne House, Queen Victoria's house on the Isle of Wight, he was astonished at the quality of some of Louise's drawings. She must have been exceptionally persuasive too because in her teens she was able to convince her mother that she should be allowed to study art – she studied at what was then known as the National Art Training School, now the Royal College of Art. But this was permitted only if she was accompanied everywhere by a chaperone.

Even with this limited freedom, Louise chafed under her mother's strict regime (a regime that echoed the Kensington System) and though she was successful to some extent in gaining a measure of artistic freedom, she was not so successful when it came to romance. Her mother was horrified when Louise fell in love with her brother's tutor – a humble vicar. The vicar was immediately sent packing, while Victoria no doubt began to search for a minor German prince.

Meanwhile, Louise made it clear that she thought her mother's permanent mourning for Albert was absurd. The two never quite fell out over this, but their relationship became strained, and it did not improve as Louise gradually began to espouse feminist views – views that horrified her mother.

Loath to lose her secretary – which is what Louise was – Victoria eventually agreed that Louise might marry an English aristocrat, though she did so in a rather begrudging way, making it very clear that no English aristocrat could possibly be compared to a German prince, however tiny his principality.

Part of what made Victoria change her mind was the growing perception that German princes were no longer popular in England – Victoria wrote to her son the Prince of Wales explaining that German princes were described in Britain as 'German beggars'.

Louise married the Marquess of Lorne in 1870 and gradually her mother's hold on her decreased, even though Victoria had only agreed to the marriage provided her daughter and new husband lived close by. One reason for the steady decline of Victoria's efforts to control Louise was that Victoria's youngest daughter Beatrice, always to some extent the favourite, had by now taken over the role of secretary and confidante, so Louise and her husband were able to escape to an apartment at Kensington Palace.

This was the apartment formerly occupied by the bibliophilic Duke of Sussex and his second wife, the Duchess of Inverness. The new occupants complained – inevitably – that everything needed to be modernised and improved. Larger rooms were created by combining smaller rooms, walls were repainted and wallpapered, furniture designed in the newly fashionable Arts and Crafts style was commissioned and Louise even created her own artist's studio by converting one of the Duke of Sussex's old libraries.

After all this work – much of it paid for by Louise from her personal fortune – her husband, Lord Lorne, was offered the post of Governor General of Canada in 1878. But the couple returned to London in 1885 and lived at Kensington until Lorne's death in 1914. Louise and her husband had not been happy and their marriage had survived only because they spent so much time apart. Despite this she was deeply affected by his death; so much so that her life as a public figure came to an end after the First World War. Increasingly reclusive, she lived on at Kensington alone for the rest of her life.

As she grew older, and with the world changing so dramatically around her, Louise seems to have recognised that the old distinctions of class and station were beginning to mean less. According to the authors of *Kensington Palace: Art, Architecture and Society*, Louise would sometimes descend to the kitchens and do her own cooking. She also developed a fondness for Isabel Porter, one of the kitchen maids. They had tea together each Friday in the kitchen office, but of course Louise would not have dreamed of inviting Isabel to tea upstairs or with her friends. The old divisions ran very deep, but Louise did far more than other princesses – when Isabel Porter fell ill with measles, Louise moved her into a room with a fireplace and sent a doctor to see her. One might ask why Isabel was in a room with no fireplace in the first place – the answer is that there was an assumption, continuing well into the twentieth century, that such luxuries as heating would 'spoil' the working classes.

Louise's cravings to escape the restrictions of life as a member of the royal family mirror those of her great-niece Princess Margaret. Louise would often hop on a bus from Kensington High Street to central London, until George V heard about it and insisted she immediately stop. He gave her an ancient Daimler, in which she could be seen for years, slowly crawling towards Knightsbridge with an elderly chauffeur at the wheel.

Louise was passionate in her support for women's suffrage and for women entering the professions. She was delighted, for example, when Elizabeth Garrett Anderson became the first woman to qualify as a doctor.

But there were sorrows in what might otherwise have been a life of ease. Her marriage to Lorne was troubled, most likely because he was predominantly homosexual. Certainly, there were no children from the marriage and there were rumours the marriage may not even have been consummated. This may well have been a trial for Louise, who faced the same societal bias as her mother and sisters – by the absurd standards of the time, well-born women were not supposed to be in the least interested in sex (beyond the needs of procreation), while their fathers and brothers, as we have seen, could and did behave as promiscuously as they pleased.

Certainly, Louise liked men, and both before and after her mother's death in 1901 she behaved with her male friends in ways that led to rumours of affairs.

She was very close to the sculptor Joseph Boehm, for example, and often worked in his studio, but London was aghast when it emerged that Louise had been alone with Boehm when the sculptor suddenly dropped dead. Inevitably people assumed that it was the exertions of sexual intercourse with the princess that had caused the sculptor's heart attack. The scandal worsened when it emerged that another sculptor, Alfred Gilbert, who had been Boehm's assistant, had agreed to destroy Boehm's papers immediately following his death. Within a short time, Gilbert was elevated to the rank of Royal Sculptor. There may have been nothing in the rumours, but the promotion of Gilbert seemed suspicious at the very least.

Louise had fallen foul of the Victorian obsession with sexual propriety; an obsession that her mother had done an enormous amount to foster. As a member of the royal family, Louise might have enjoyed a materially rich life, but she also had to adhere to impossibly rigid moral codes that included going nowhere and seeing no one while unaccompanied. Because she liked to go about as she pleased, other rumours sprang up – she was even said to have had an affair with the architect Edwin Lutyens, but for this there is no real evidence.

But Louise did have a secret life – she often went under the pseudonym Mrs Campbell and, knowing she was hardly likely to be recognised in her everyday clothes, she would slip out of Kensington Palace undetected and do as she liked.

Living alone at Kensington, especially after her mother's death, certainly increased both her eccentricities and her rebelliousness – she was a chain smoker, loved the company of her womanising brother Edward VII, and believed in intensive exercise for women at a time when any exercise for well-born women was considered highly dangerous. When she was told that her exercise regime would do her no good at all, she would reply, 'Ah. Well, I will outlive you all.' And that, to a large extent, is exactly what she did.

Like other minor royals at Kensington, Louise had other houses to which she could retreat when London became a bore. Her mother had given her Kent House in the grounds of Osborne House on the Isle of Wight, but she also spent time at her husband's home, Inveraray Castle in Scotland.

Judith Morris's mother, Edith, worked for Louise for several years at Kensington Palace in the 1920s and Judith remembered her mother explaining Louise's curious mix of high-handedness and kindness, coarseness and obsessive refinement.

My mother worked for Louise for about five years, I think, and like most servants at that time she felt her mistress could do no wrong – she was a member of the royal family and therefore beyond criticism – but some of the things Mum told me revealed that Louise, at least in her later years, was eccentric to the point of being completely potty.

Sometimes she spoke to Mum as if she (Mum) was a robot – no please or thank you, no eye contact, no smiles. But despite this Mum felt a little sorry for Louise because she could do almost nothing for herself – she would ring a bell and my mother would dutifully go along the servants' passageways, carefully avoiding the main staircases, which in all her time she neither saw nor used. Usually Mum would be summoned because Louise had mislaid her cigarettes, or needed a cushion for her back, or wanted a curtain drawn or a window opened.

Mum told me Louise adored cigarettes and smoked almost continually, but she would leave the cigarettes all over the place, sometimes still alight. Mum said it was a wonder the palace didn't burn down. Louise also disliked her sister Beatrice, who lived in the apartment next door to Louise's. Mum would hear shouting late in the evening and assumed it was the two sisters arguing through the walls. Louise also liked a drink, too, and when she was tipsy, she would bang on her sister's wall and shout abuse. Mum thought the smoking and drinking came about because Louise had most of her fun in the company of her brother and his numerous drinking and smoking friends, who were all very disreputable, but he'd been dead since 1910 so she missed the fun of those years. Like all Victoria's children, Louise had been overly controlled for so long by her tyrannical mother that when she died, they all went slightly mad with relief – also grief, of course, but they were suddenly free. Everyone was convinced, for example, that Louise really did have lovers when she was younger, and Mum insisted rumours persisted into Louise's sixties and seventies because an endless series of what Mum called 'artistic types' used to visit Louise at the palace. Mum said that whatever Louise got up to when she was young, she certainly wasn't doing anything she shouldn't have done by this stage – she just liked the company of artistic types because they drank and smoked and said outrageous things.

Louise used to apologise to Mum for being so impractical and would mutter about the difficulty of getting dressed if her maid was absent for any reason. She used to say, 'Clothes really are the most beastly things, so dreadfully complicated. How is one supposed to manage?'

But Mum insisted Louise could be very kind: you couldn't ask for time off if you were a servant in those days just because you didn't feel well, so when she started coming down with flu, feeling very weak, Mum continued to work. Louise soon noticed something was wrong and ordered her to bed, where a footman brought her soup and bowls of hot water for the next few days until she was better. Louise even turned up in Mum's bedroom to make sure she was improving. She offered a cigarette in what was meant to be a kindly tone but came across as rather bossy – because Louise was famously bossy. She said, 'Do buck up. You are more than capable of dealing with these Germans.' (My mother always insisted she said 'Germans', but in her confusion she probably misheard the word 'germs'!)

One of Mum's favourite stories about Louise – although I'm not sure my mother wasn't exaggerating when she told it – was the time when, on leaving the palace one summer afternoon, she saw Louise hanging out of a window with a cigarette in her mouth and suddenly shouting to one of the gardeners, 'Stop walking across that fucking flower bed!' She also had a very odd habit of making drawings of her lunch and dinner and sending them down to the cook!

In her last years, Louise became religious and began almost obsessively to compose lengthy prayers, which she carefully posted to various members of the then government. When she knew she was dying, she donned her old wedding veil. She died aged ninety-one in her bedroom at Kensington and was cremated – as she had asked to be in her will – at Golders Green Crematorium. Her ashes were placed in a vault at the royal burial ground at Frogmore near Windsor.

Louise's lasting legacy is the magnificent statue of her mother outside the East Front of Kensington Palace, for which she made the maquette.

But what of Princess Beatrice, Louise's neighbour at Kensington? Beatrice, the last child of Queen Victoria, was born in 1857. She lived at Kensington Palace from 1896 until her death in 1944. When she was young, Beatrice probably assumed she would never leave her mother, for she was the last of Victoria's children and very obviously the favourite child. Like her older sisters, she became her mother's secretary and companion – but unlike the other sisters, who could comfort themselves with the thought that another sister was always waiting in the wings to take over, Beatrice knew that there was no one to take her place. She seems to have accepted this with good grace – indeed, she seems almost to have relished the idea of staying with her mother and having no independent life of her own. But that all changed when she met Prince Henry of Battenberg (1858–96).

When Beatrice told her mother that she wished to marry Henry, the queen was so shocked that she refused to speak to her daughter for six months.

Beatrice worked hard to convince Victoria that she should be allowed to marry and eventually a compromise was reached that was rather similar to Victoria's compromise with her daughter Louise. Louise, we may recall, had to agree to live *close* to her mother with her new husband; Beatrice had to agree that she would live permanently with the queen at Buckingham Palace.

Beatrice and Henry were married in 1885 and enjoyed a short but apparently very happy marriage. Henry died of malaria in 1896 while returning from the Fourth Anglo-Ashanti War of 1895. Beatrice was inconsolable and went into a month-long period of isolation and mourning. Without her husband, it was felt that Beatrice needed somewhere of her own to live. Victoria gave her the apartment at

Kensington where she herself had lived with her mother, the Duchess of Kent. From 1896 until 1901, when her mother finally died, Beatrice returned to her secretarial duties. She spent an astonishing thirty years transcribing and then destroying her mother's huge collection of diaries – more than two thirds of all the original diaries were destroyed during this process, inevitably leading to speculation that the diaries contained considerable quantities of possibly hurtful and indiscreet material.

Given that Victoria was hugely narcissistic, self-pitying and self-dramatising she would certainly have included a great deal in the diaries that others might have found inappropriate. The entries covering the period during which Victoria appears to have been deeply in love with her Scottish gillie John Brown were almost certainly deeply shocking. It may be, as a number of Victoria's biographers have argued, that her passion for Brown was entirely platonic. On the other hand, her most recent biographer A. N. Wilson suggests that the Scottish clergyman Dr Norman MacLeod may well have performed a marriage ceremony of some kind for Victoria and Brown at Balmoral. We know that Victoria was a sensual woman, and the marriage service, if indeed it took place, would have been designed to ensure that Victoria could sleep with Brown without offending her sense of decorum. Nothing significant of the relationship with Brown survived Beatrice's editing.

The destruction of so many of her mother's diaries suggests that Beatrice was horrified by what she uncovered. But the relationship with Brown could not be entirely hidden – its intensity can be judged by the fact that Victoria insisted that Brown's portrait should be buried with her – held in her dead hand, in fact – rather than Albert's.

Unlike Louise, Beatrice did not enjoy the company of her brother Edward VII. She disapproved of his philandering, his life of self-indulgence.

Beatrice's biographer Matthew Dennison suggests that she was far more interested in the lives of the poor than her siblings were. She was especially concerned about conditions in Britain's coalmines, but though she spoke out on the subject she did nothing practical about it. She divided her time between her apartment at Kensington Palace (where she tried to avoid meeting her sister as much as possible), a house at East Cowes on the Isle of Wight and Brantridge Park in West Sussex, owned by the Earl of Athlone.

Horrified that Germany and Britain should find themselves at war in 1914, she gave up all her German titles. To this disaster must be added the death of her son Maurice, who was killed in action at Ypres. For the last twenty years of her life she became more reclusive. She had been a brilliant pianist as a young woman and no doubt deeply regretted that her royal status made it impossible for her to play for anyone but friends and family.

According to her daughter Judith, Edith Morris remembered hearing the melancholy sounds of Beatrice playing the piano alone in her apartment at Kensington, but her arthritic fingers made this increasingly difficult. Edith also recalled that Beatrice was gentler and less demanding than her sister Louise.

Mum told me that Beatrice, who was only at Kensington for part of each year, would sit staring out of the window for hours. Her shyness turned into a definite streak of reclusiveness that probably had a lot to do with not liking the way the world had changed. Mum thought she had never recovered from the shock of her son Maurice's death in the war, and she disliked the modern world anyway – Britain's war with Germany was inexplicable to her. She would grumble that we really should not have allowed ourselves to become so silly about Germany. She would mumble to herself, 'Absurd. Poor Germany. They are our friends, indeed our family. Ridiculous.' Then moments later she would say, 'Carriages are really so much more civilised.'

Beatrice died at the Earl of Athlone's house at Brantridge in 1944, from where she was taken to the Isle of Wight for burial. Like most of Kensington Palace's residents, she had left for the countryside when war broke out. She was the last of Victoria's children to die and, astonishingly, her death occurred almost seventy years after that of her first sibling.

CHAPTER THIRTEEN

FAT MARY

'Her size is fearful.'
QUEEN VICTORIA

Perhaps the most colourful character at Kensington Palace in the second half of the nineteenth century was George III's granddaughter Princess Mary Adelaide, Duchess of Cambridge. She was given an apartment at Kensington in the late 1860s and her four children – three boys and a girl – were born at the palace.

She is remembered, more than anything, for her enormous bulk – she was known affectionately as 'Fat Mary' by the British public and seems to have been incredibly popular, her size being seen to indicate a fun-loving, reckless character. Her reputation for fun was certainly justified if one is to judge by reports of the huge parties she hosted. Indeed, these were so extravagant and held so frequently that despite her large annual grant from the Treasury, she and her husband, Francis of Teck, had to leave Britain in 1883 to escape their debts. They owed around £18,000 and had asked Queen Victoria to pay the money. The queen refused and they left the country after the sale of all their furniture and household goods.

Strangely, 'Fat Mary' was criticised only a little for her extravagance – like Edward VII, her high living seemed almost refreshing to a public grown bored of the gloomy puritanism of Queen Victoria and her inner circle.

The irony was that ordinary people who could not afford to leave the country to escape their creditors were still being sent to prison at this time. The tradesmen of Kensington – florists, butchers, greengrocers and so on – knew that supplying the royal residents of Kensington Palace with goods on credit was both unavoidable (royalty only ever paid when they felt like it) and risky, because as in the case of Mary of Teck, they might just disappear. The risks were deemed worth taking as supplying the palace was both prestigious and, if the goods were paid for, lucrative.

Edward Callaghan's great-grandfather ran a small general shop in Kensington at this time.

The family story was that shopkeepers all over Kensington were delighted and depressed at the same time when they received a large regular order from the palace. Residents were so grand that they expected shopkeepers to keep supplying their goods on almost indefinite credit – usually the bills were paid in the end, but sometimes not. You could hardly prosecute a member of the royal family at that time for debt. You just wouldn't dare.

Mary and her husband returned to London in 1885 and lived a little more quietly – it is easy to imagine the dressing-down they would have received from Victoria, who intensely disliked anything that might be perceived as damaging the family's reputation. But Mary was a key figure in the royal family – she was the mother of Mary of Teck (1867–1953), who in turn became the wife of King George V.

Mary Adelaide and her husband had been allocated the apartment that had once been home to Victoria and her mother. References to 'apartments' may give the impression that the relatives of Victoria were living in a palace subdivided into rather small units of accommodation – in fact, almost all those allowed to live at Kensington were housed in something far bigger than the average London terrace. Princess Mary Adelaide is a case in point – her 'apartment' took up three floors and looked out across the park towards the Serpentine. This was probably the loveliest view from any home in London. She and her husband enjoyed the use of more than eighty rooms. Princess Alice, who, as has been mentioned, lived at Kensington until 1981, lived in an apartment with more than 100 rooms.

When they were first given their apartment, Mary and her husband felt it would be 'simply impossible' to move in until the Office of Works had paid for significant improvements and modernisation. Queen Victoria often visited Mary and she must have felt nostalgia, perhaps mixed with sadness, to see her old apartment lived in by others who were determined to erase any traces of the past.

From the restrained elegance of the Georgian interiors, the new residents transformed their apartments so that they took on the cluttered, typically Victorian and rather sombre appearance we associate with the interiors of the last part of the nineteenth century. Tables and mantelpieces (of which there were many) were covered with photographs and bibelots, snuffboxes, cigarette cases, ornaments and curiosities;

there were large plants and vases of flowers everywhere. The walls were covered with paintings in heavy gilt frames.

The six members of Mary's family found it hard to survive without their twenty-eight regular servants, who were housed in small rooms in the basement.

Judith Morris's mother recalled these rooms from her time at the palace in the 1930s.

Mum told me there was an unwritten rule that servants would cease to be good servants if they got a taste for luxuries or comfortable living – such things were inappropriate to their station in life – so servants' rooms at Kensington and elsewhere were incredibly spartan. It wasn't exactly that the royals were mean or unkind, but more that they had inherited ideas about servants and how to treat them that really dated back to George III and perhaps beyond. There was a general belief that servants were almost like children who had to be controlled. Mum said, 'We had to have things that were appropriate to our station in life and at the time we just accepted this without questioning it – so in my room at Kensington I had a plain deal washstand, a few hooks to hang my clothes, a simple iron bedstead and a small rug. Some of my fellow servants didn't have the rug and were very jealous – and maids often didn't even have fireplaces. In very cold weather they would sleep in their clothes. I don't think I had my rug for any reason other than they needed somewhere to put it! Lots of things at Kensington seemed to have been put in odd places just to store them. In fact, many corridors and rooms had stacks of old pictures and bits of beautiful broken furniture left lying about. You might think they'd have at least put a picture or two on the servants' walls, but they didn't because they assumed we had no interest or knowledge – I think they thought of it as giving a book to someone who couldn't read. It was that sort of idea rather than cruelty or insensitivity. I sometimes thought perhaps they imagined we'd steal the pictures – mind you, that would have been difficult as most of the old pictures lying about were massive!'

Like Marie Antoinette, who liked to play at being a humble shepherdess, Mary Adelaide liked occasionally to dress as a servant to amuse her dinner guests; it was the absurdity of the idea of a royal being a servant that amused – like transforming gold into lead.

❧

In addition to her relatives, Queen Victoria gave grace-and-favour apartments – almost invariably for life – to upper-class servants, including, for example, Lady Caroline Barrington, a Woman of the Bedchamber who had helped looked after Victoria's children. The tradition of giving apartments to loyal servants applied only to those who were aristocratic, or at the very least upper class, and it was a tradition that was unchanged by the mid-twentieth century when, for example, Lady Bertha Dawkins, a former lady-in-waiting to Queen Mary of Teck, was still in residence. By this time the larger apartments had sometimes been turned into smaller apartments – so that there were more of them – and the stables and other service rooms had been converted into further apartments. Almost all were given not to members of the immediate royal family but to women and men like Bertha Dawkins and others who were well off and, in most cases, had their own houses elsewhere. But that, of course, is to miss the point…

Probably until as recently as the 1950s, even relatively distant members of the royal family lived at Kensington Palace at the taxpayers' expense because the public longed for the fantasy that at least one family in Britain should live a life of medieval splendour; and medieval splendour included the idea that the monarch could and should dispense largesse in exactly the way medieval monarchs did. William of Normandy gave land and titles to his family and friends; modern monarchs give grace-and-favour apartments.

With the death of Queen Victoria's last child, Princess Beatrice, in 1944, perhaps the best-known of the immediate family members living at Kensington in the second half of the twentieth century was Princess Alice, the last grandchild of Victoria. Alice, who lived to be ninety-seven, died at Kensington in 1981. She had moved out with most of the other residents during the Second World War but was back by 1946, as her apartments were only slightly damaged. Other apartments had not fared so well after an incendiary bomb destroyed a major part of the roof in 1940 – the impact was enough to make at least six of the ten apartments temporarily uninhabitable.

Perhaps sensing that the world was changing, Alice was often seen wandering alone in Kensington Gardens or shopping in Kensington High Street, although the story about her first unaccompanied visit to a shop is probably apocryphal: she was apparently astonished to discover that you had to pay if you wanted to take anything away with you. But this new world of cars and lorries and increasing egalitarianism must have seemed alien to her.

Her greatest tragedy perhaps had occurred during the First World War, at the outbreak of which she had to relinquish all her German titles. Worse still, her brother fought on the German side and was stripped of his British titles by an Act of Parliament. In the Second World War he became a Nazi sympathiser, although he was by no means the only member of the royal family to feel some sympathy towards a regime that believed in a master race.

After the end of the Second World War, and despite protests from many members of the new Labour government – elected in a landslide victory in July 1945 – the damaged parts of Kensington Palace were slowly repaired and modernised so that the various residents who had escaped to the countryside for the duration could move back in.

Various parts of the building were turned into servants' flats, and the tiny rooms where they had formerly lived gradually became a thing of the past. Curiously, the word 'flats' seems always to be used when writers discuss servants' quarters; the more genteel word 'apartments' is always used for the residents' accommodation.

Many Labour MPs were angry that, given the severe shortage of housing after the war, so much money was spent creating and modifying housing for the extended royal family and their equerries and ladies-in-waiting. But old habits of deference die hard, as we have seen.

Ron Wilson, who worked at the palace in the 1960s, says that lots of the servants were baffled by the range of people who lived there, many of whom seemed to be entirely unknown to each other and only very distantly related to the royal family.

He said:

The aristocratic servants who had smart rooms or even houses in the palace grounds – actually they weren't really servants at all – tended to stay for years so they knew everyone, were very well paid and had aristocratic backgrounds and their own houses or estates outside London. But those of us at the bottom of the pile, the cleaners and maids and kitchen staff, tended to stay a shorter time because we were paid very little, and we either lived out, or lived 'in' but in spartan conditions.

There were well-known residents such as Princess Alice – who was completely batty in the way only old aristocratic women can be – but there were a number of other elderly people with wonderfully clipped accents around the place and we barely knew who they were or why they were there. They would always speak in a commanding voice, so no one thought to question whether they should even have been there – we used to joke that so long as they sounded right, and were self-assured enough, they could have just walked in off the street and no one would have said a word.

Some were quite mad – I remember one old lady took me by the arm one evening and began talking to me about a dance she had been to before the war. I thought she meant the Second War but quickly realised she meant World War I. From the way she talked, it was also obvious that despite my London accent she thought I was somehow connected to her early life – and not as a servant. She even gossiped in a low voice about the sexual appetites of Edward VII. She would lean in close to me and say, 'And do you know, the little bastard hardly had a bath in his life. Absolutely stank. And do you know, he only went with women who'd had their hands on every man in London.' She started every sentence, 'And do you know…'

I would smile and listen but it was very embarrassing and I could have been sacked for talking to her, except of course I had no choice and if I'd walked away brusquely and she'd turned Turk I'd have been sacked anyway. But I have no idea who she was.

Everyone knew the war had made people's lives difficult, but in the main, the royal family (or rather, that bit of it that lived at Kensington) expected their own lives to carry on as they were before the war. It took them a while to realise things had changed, some never realised, or they refused to accept it. I remember one old lady complaining that she hated labour-saving devices – she refused to have her linen washed in a machine, so a maid was given the job of washing it every week. The residents all still expected the tradesmen round about to deliver their food and drink and cigarettes. Many of them had no practical abilities at all. They thought things arrived as if by magic.

This is something with which the former maid Rose Plummer would have agreed:

After the Second World War there was a strange sort of shift in relations where some employers who'd never looked after themselves and didn't know how to do it were terrified that if they weren't nice to their servants, especially their cooks and maids, they would lose them. Lots of little old ladies who thought servants would always be there to do everything for them were soon going to be either eating beans out of tins or learning to open and close the oven door!

Suddenly relations between many old ladies and their maids began to soften and the old ladies would be nice and trot down for tea in the maid's room or housekeeper's room, a thing that would never have happened before the war. Of course, this happened less often the further up the social scale you went – royal princesses were always likely to be able to get servants because of the prestige of working for the royal family. But even they knew that the days when you could treat the servants as if they were machines or animals were over – if we got upset, we could get a job somewhere else. By the 1950s and '60s, factories and shops all over London let us escape, if we wanted, from the shame of 'cap and apron', as it used to be called.

Among those whose apartments needed major work to repair bomb damage was Derek Keppel – a descendant of those Keppels we saw working for King William and King George nearly three centuries earlier. The first Keppel's rapid promotion to an earldom led to speculation that he and William were lovers. And if that scandal were not enough, the Sir Derek Keppel who lived at the palace until his death in 1944 was related to George Keppel, the cuckolded husband of Alice Keppel, Edward VII's most notorious mistress. These connections were never seen as sullied by adultery or scandal of any kind. For the royals, making a fuss about these things is distinctly and embarrassingly suburban.

Other royals awaiting apartments in the palace as repairs and modernisation continued after the war included Princess Marina, Duchess of Kent (1906–68), who was Greek, and her three children; also the Marquess of Carisbrooke (son of Princess Beatrice), Princess Andrew of Greece, the Dowager Marchioness of Milford Haven, and Prince Philip, who lived at Kensington Palace with Princess Elizabeth for a short time after their marriage in 1947.

Princess Marina was only just prevented from destroying an original Wren staircase – she disliked it because it was 'too much like a servant's staircase', by which she meant it was too narrow for her to descend in full evening dress without her dress touching the sides.

Alan 'Tommy' Lascelles, who became famous (or notorious) for ruthlessly opposing Princess Margaret's marriage to Group Captain Townsend, was offered an apartment in the old stables at Kensington on his retirement in 1953; Deputy Treasurer to the Queen Sir Dudley Colles moved into a refurbished cottage in the grounds; Master of the Horse, the Duke of Beaufort, one of Britain's richest men, was given an apartment, as was Sir Ivan de la Bere, who enjoyed the splendid title Secretary General of the Central Chancery of the Orders of Knighthood. Despite his title, the Master of the Horse is only rarely found at Knightsbridge Barracks mucking out the stables. The duties of the Secretary General of the Central Chancery of the Orders of Knighthood are equally difficult to fathom, but in the late 1940s, as London was slowly being rebuilt, his presence in London – like that of the Duke of Beaufort – was deemed vital, and so they came to live at Kensington.

Most of these people had been born when Queen Victoria was still alive, and as they died, we gradually move into the modern era and a new (and perhaps less stuffy) generation of royals that famously includes Catherine Middleton, the first genuine commoner to marry an heir to the throne. Other contenders for the title of 'first commoner', such as Anne Boleyn, were actually aristocrats. The American divorcee Meghan Markle represents an even more significant move away from the traditions of British royalty. Americans have long married into the British aristocracy – most famously, perhaps, Sir Winston Churchill's mother was an American – but it will be remembered that an American divorcee also caused a king to abdicate. Meghan Markle's arrival at Kensington Palace caused not a few raised eyebrows and internal wrangles that led eventually to her departure for Windsor with husband Prince Harry. More recent developments in the lives of the royal couple and their son have caused a damaging rift – the most damaging in a generation – within the royal family, a subject covered in the final chapter of this book.

The fact that there was no longer a Tommy Lascelles to rail against royals marrying commoners or divorcees speaks volumes about changes in the royal family and social attitudes in general. But there is a pragmatic element to this – the first consideration for the royal family is survival, and pushing against the tide of egalitarianism is no longer an option in the twenty-first century. The view at Kensington and Buckingham Palace has been that allowing this generation of young royals to marry commoners will persuade the public that the royal family is aware of the need for change. Meghan and Kate are also, as it were, a welcome distraction – if they are there, then it is easier for the rest of the royal apparatus to continue as before, with dukes, earls and Old Etonians being offered sinecures and highly paid roles as equerries, Masters of the Stole and Mistresses of the Robes.

Richard Lewis (not his real name), who worked at Kensington Palace until recently, said:

The fact that Kate and Meghan have been allowed to marry into the family does not mean that the Queen would consider for a moment offering to employ an ordinary woman as, for example, Mistress of the Robes – that job always goes to an aristocrat. The Queen just doesn't feel comfortable with people outside the circle she has known all her life. It's no coincidence that the Duke of Norfolk is her best friend or that all her senior ceremonial appointments are aristocrats. For her, Meghan and Kate are exercises in public relations. She is far cannier than you might think and like most old people she hates change – which is not to say that she doesn't like Meghan or Kate. She adores them, but she isn't comfortable with them the way she is with the sort of people she has been surrounded by all her life – from her time as a little girl, when no one would have questioned the right of the royal family to appoint aristocrats to every significant role. She grew up with that and she is nostalgic about it. But also, as I have said – pragmatic.

As we will see, many of the most dramatic changes to the royal family's attitudes can be attributed to the woman who might easily be described as the most significant royal of the past century: Diana, Princess of Wales.

CHAPTER FOURTEEN

FUCK YOU, TOO!

'I have no intention of telling people what I have for breakfast.'
PRINCESS MARGARET

As the modern royals have arrived, so Kensington Palace has undergone further modernisation – the younger royals are almost more of a heritage attraction than the palace itself, and in keeping with this, the palace is soon to receive (or suffer) its most intrusive modernisation ever. A plan has been drawn up to create a vast suite of offices running underground between the old palace and the Orangery. Critics have condemned the cost and the disturbance to an important historical site and asked if it is really necessary to create a vast communications empire for Kate and William and their children. Do they really need an enormous communications team and scores of personal servants, nannies and footmen?

But whatever the criticisms, William and Kate are adding to the structure rather than damaging what is already there (assuming the Orangery doesn't collapse as the huge basement is dug out beneath it).

Previous generations of royals have not had the same consideration for the historic fabric of the house. Among the most destructive Kensington Palace residents were Princess Margaret and Lord Snowdon.

The story of Princess Margaret's relationship with Group Captain Townsend (1914–95) is too well known to need repeating here. Suffice it to say that Margaret was forbidden to marry under the Royal Marriages Act of 1772 on pain of losing her rank and privileges. Townsend was banished to Belgium to ensure the couple were kept well apart. Some time later, Margaret received a letter from Townsend, saying he intended to marry. Margaret was so upset that the very next day she accepted a proposal from photographer Antony Armstrong-Jones (1930–2017). The marriage was a disaster almost from the outset. It was also arguably a disaster for Kensington Palace. According to a former servant, the marriage put Margaret in a bad temper with everyone for the rest of her life. Margaret's lady-in-waiting, Lady Glenconner, confessed in her memoirs that the Queen's sister was even capable of taking out her anger on her enemies' pets – Lady Glenconner was asked to chase Prince and Princess Michael's cats round the garden with a hose or to try to run them over.

Armstrong-Jones, later Lord Snowdon, was a devoted modernist who also considered himself a talented designer. As a result, he insisted on being involved in the remodelling of Apartment 1A at Kensington Palace. The Ministry of Works agreed to do the work and foot the bill, but Armstrong-Jones's designs were very much in accord with the aesthetic values of the 1960s – values that very quickly went out of date.

As a result, some of the oldest parts of the palace that had been designed by Christopher Wren were destroyed – the vaults under the Stone Gallery, for example, were completely demolished; early decorative schemes were obliterated; fireplaces and panelling ended up in the skip; the Duke of Sussex's beautifully made bookcases were burned; internal walls were removed and new partitions created. The new young couple also found it impossible to manage without a lift. As a *Times* journalist put it, 'A Wren masterpiece is being turned into something one might expect to see at the Daily Mail Ideal Home Exhibition.' The ultimate irony was that having ripped out most of the original work, Princess Margaret and Lord Snowdon (or rather, the taxpayer) spent a fortune introducing faux eighteenth-century décor.

Photographs of the couple's new kitchen, designed by Snowdon himself, show a dull, spartan-looking series of Formica-covered cupboards that a *Punch* journalist described at the time as 'council house chic'. And we know how frequently modernisation leads to regret and reinstatement of what was originally there – in the 1970s, for example, when preserving the past was becoming a priority, William Kent fireplaces were taken out of storage at Kensington Palace, where they'd lain dusty and forgotten for thirty years, to be reinstated in apartments created for Charles and Diana. The fireplaces had been removed in the 1930s as part of an earlier process of 'modernisation'. Lord Snowdon's super-modern kitchen, as it happens, has long since been demolished.

Much of what we remember today of Princess Margaret and Antony Armstrong-Jones is, sadly, the fury and anguish of their years together. Like most tragic relationships, theirs had its amusing moments. Their habit, for example, of leaving notes here and there around their

Kensington apartment, saying such things as, 'Here are ten reasons why I hate you…'

Ron Wilson remembers 'blistering rows' that could be heard all over the palace.

She [Princess Margaret] would shriek the most terrible things and she didn't give a damn if the windows and doors were open and everyone could hear. Quite a shock, I can tell you, to hear the queen's sister shout the word 'cunt' at the top of her voice. I think she'd only learned it by mixing with her husband's bohemian friends. If you'd asked me, I'd have said there was no way she'd have known that word, but she did.

A lot of their rows were based on the fact that they competed to see who could sleep with the greatest number of people – it was a sort of tit-for-tat. She'd have sex with someone and flaunt it at him, so he'd go off and do the same and let her know. Once, I believe she slept with one of his male friends and then he deliberately slept with the same man! So, when she shouted, 'I fucked your friend so and so…' he shot back, 'So did I.' I think he usually won these battles because she was always stumped when he told her he'd had sex with a man. I don't think she had sex with women – although there were rumours among the staff!

Following the couple's divorce in 1978, Margaret lived on alone at Kensington. She was variously portrayed in the press as either a sad, lonely woman or a chain-smoking virago – the latter description gaining the upper hand as a result of life among the jet-set, and then her long-term relationship with the much younger Roddy Llewellyn (born in 1947). When the relationship began in 1973, she was forty-three and he twenty-five.

Princess Margaret's enormous apartment became a focus for the artistic – some would say 'louche' – people whose company she had craved since her youth. There's little doubt that it was Armstrong-Jones's lifestyle among *Vogue* models, fashion designers, painters and photographers that captivated Margaret – marriage to Armstrong-Jones meant a ticket to a drug- and alcohol-fuelled lifestyle in which people seemed to have endless fun; it was a lifestyle that contrasted with her own existence, which she saw as hidebound and restrictive, overly controlled and dull.

Of course, she could have abandoned her life and privileges as a princess and married Townsend, but much as she longed for another world away from royal life there was a part of her that clung to the privileges and status of her position. When in later life she mixed with Roddy Llewellyn, Cleo Lane, Noël Coward, Elizabeth Taylor, Mary Quant and others, she felt she was one of them – truly artistic. It's possible that it was only when she was partying, and drinking increasingly heavily, that she could feel happy. This could lead to very embarrassing moments, as Ron Wilson recalled:

I remember once I was serving drinks at one of her parties in Apartment 1A and she had got up to sing. Everyone stood around the piano while she sang a standard jazz number – I can't remember exactly what – and while she was singing, I made sure I stood quite still. She would have given me hell afterwards if I had carried on round the room. She expected total attention from everyone when she was performing.

Anyway, even I could tell that she could not really sing a note – she was out of tune and her timing wasn't that great either. The pianist, who was really good, did his best to cover for her (and keep up with her), but it was hopeless. It might have been the fact that she was drunk, but even sober she was not as good a singer as she thought she was. At the end, of course everyone roared their approval and applauded wildly. She was delighted. She felt she was one among the artists. But she couldn't see that she would not have received such a rapturous reception had she not been the queen's sister. All her life, I think she must have been praised when the praise wasn't really meant, so she couldn't tell what was fake from what was real; because, you see, for her there was no real. She was praised, whatever she did, because of who she was. And this worked both ways – even if she was good at something (something other than singing!) she could never be sure if people really were praising her abilities. On the other hand, she was very insecure and would have had a nervous breakdown trying to deal with any criticism of any kind. She was so convinced she had real talent – like her so-called friends – that she would have found it unbearable not to be praised.

Wilson's analysis is confirmed by an account given by the writer and journalist Daniel Farson in his memoir, *The Gilded Gutter Life of Francis Bacon*. As a star of the art world, Bacon had been invited to one of the princess's parties. At some point she stood up to perform her usual party trick of singing, egged on by the sycophantic audience. Bacon was drunk and didn't care that she was the queen's sister, and he began shouting abuse at her as she sang – he bellowed that she couldn't sing a note. A shocked silence fell on the room. Margaret stopped abruptly, flushed, and then stormed out of the room, her face crimson with rage.

Journalist and writer Craig Brown's brilliantly funny book about Princess Margaret, *Ma'am Darling*, sums up her situation perfectly:

> Someone who was an occasional guest at [Kenneth] Tynan's soirees told me that the assembled bohemians – actors, writers, artists, musicians – would kowtow to her royal highness while she was present and then make fun of her the moment she left, mimicking her general ignorance, her cack-handed opinions, her lofty put-downs, her absurd air of entitlement. The presence of the princess would endow a party with grandeur; her departure would be the signal for mimicry to commence. Beside these laughing sophisticates, the princess could sometimes appear an innocent.

Then again, she was also famously rude and cutting, so it is difficult to feel sympathy for her. Brown recalls another incident when the film producer Robert Evans attended the premiere of the film *Love Story*, on which Evans had worked. He lined up to meet Princess Margaret. She shook his hand and said, 'Tony saw *Love Story* in New York. Hated it.' before stalking off. Evans responded (presumably sotto voce), 'Fuck you, too.'

But Margaret's problem, whether at her own parties at Kensington Palace or elsewhere, was simply that she was unfulfilled and unhappy; and as the writer Elizabeth Bowen pointed out about Virginia Woolf, who was rather similar to Princess Margaret in many ways, 'She was frightening because she was frightened.'

Chain-smoking, heavy drinking and profound discontent led to the early death of Princess Margaret aged seventy-one in 2002. She was taken from her apartment at Kensington to Slough Crematorium to be cremated. It was a final act of defiance in which she refused a traditional burial at Windsor, although her ashes were later placed next to her father's coffin in St George's Chapel. But like earlier disaffected royals – most notably Queen Victoria's 'wicked uncle' the Duke of Sussex – Margaret was determined to avoid anything that might look even remotely like a state funeral.

CHAPTER FIFTEEN

LOVE AMONG THE RUINS

'When you are happy, you can forgive a great deal.'
DIANA, PRINCESS OF WALES

When Prince Charles and Lady Diana Spencer married in 1981, they moved into an extraordinary apartment in Kensington Palace – extraordinary because it was in fact two apartments, known as 8 and 9. The most heavily war-damaged of all Kensington's apartments, these had been rebuilt in the 1970s and were then updated for Prince Charles in 1979.

Every generation of royals calls in the fashionable architects and designers of the day – in the seventeenth and eighteenth centuries it was William Kent and Capability Brown; in the mid-twentieth century it was the theatre designer Carl Toms (favoured by Princess Margaret); in the 1980s it was an interior designer called Dudley Poplak.

Using pictures and furniture from the Royal Collection, Poplak created a sort of pastiche of Georgian elegance across the whole of

Apartments 8 and 9. After Charles's marriage to Diana, more space was required – presumably because it was assumed the couple would have children. In traditional royal fashion, a whole suite of rooms on the second floor was given over to a nursery – it needed to be a suite to accommodate the babies and their staff; on the ground floor below the royal couple were the servants' quarters and numerous offices.

Various books have recounted the memories of those who support-ed Diana as the world's most glamorous marriage began to fall apart. Much of what has been written concentrates on Diana's unhappiness, her bulimia and her romantic liaisons after her divorce. Less has been written about how Kensington Palace and its gardens became an almost physical solace for the princess.

The central difficulty of the marriage – a difficulty that long predated the actual marriage itself – was that Charles was and is, in many ways, a throwback to his Hanoverian ancestors. Like George I and George II (not to mention the 'wicked uncles'), he seems to have assumed that the heir to the throne was entitled to have a mistress or several and that it was not his wife's place to complain. It is a story we have seen again and again: monarchs without political power tend to try to exert too much personal power. Charles felt he was too important to be told what to do by anyone, but least of all his wife. Diana, on the other hand, had a more modern view of marriage, seeing it as a partnership of equals who remained loyal to each other and certainly didn't sleep with other people. Charles's marriage had darker antecedents, as a recent biography of Edward VII's mistress Mrs Keppel shows:

Above all things, Alice Keppel loved money and position. Her values and attitudes were passed down in their purest form to Camilla, Duchess of Cornwall, formerly Camilla Parker Bowles, who effectively destroyed the marriage between Charles, Prince of Wales, and Lady Diana Spencer.

Camilla Shand, as she then was, grew up in an atmosphere in which affairs were treated much as her great-grandmother Alice Keppel's circle treated them: they were private matters with no moral aspect at all. And thus, when Camilla said to Charles in 1970, 'My great-grandmother was the mistress of your great-great-grandfather so how about it?' she no doubt simply thought this was carrying on an exciting royal tradition; a tradition that says morality, like taxes, is for little people.

Camilla's affair with Charles continued before, during and after his marriage to Diana Spencer and, shockingly, Camilla even helped Charles buy Highgrove House, still his home today, because it was close to the house she shared with her husband. It was a shrewd move of which Camilla's great-grandmother would have approved.

Knowing that as a divorced woman – and definitely not a virgin – she would not be allowed to marry Charles, Camilla advised him to marry Lady Diana Spencer. Camilla thought this would be a good idea as the perception was that Diana was timid, easily led and therefore unlikely to make a fuss when she discovered that Charles had no intention of giving up his mistress. Diana was to be his brood mare.

This was the backdrop to Diana's famous statement, given in a television interview, that her marriage had been a bit crowded as three people were involved.

The discovery that her husband was and had been cheating on her both before and during the earliest days of her marriage was a tremendous shock, and the battles that ensued while Charles tried to carry on as if having a mistress was his birthright and Diana really shouldn't be making a fuss were conducted in those beautifully refurbished apartments at Kensington. According to one former Kensington Palace servant, the marriage did not even have a happy start. Charles was emotionally absent even before the marriage, which he saw as a dynastic necessity – but one that gave him little pleasure.

There is a myth that Charles and Diana were living happily in this beautiful palace, at least for their first few years together, but actually you could hear them rowing almost from the day they moved in. Poor old Charles had had a terrible time at school – he was bullied, as we know, and made to feel unmanly – so once he reached adulthood he was going to be in charge; if he wanted something, he felt other people, and that included his wife, should simply accept that he should have it.

The trouble was he was heir to the throne, and it's very hard when everyone kowtows to you, and gives you the impression that you really are a very special person, to suddenly find that you are up against someone who wants to be treated as an equal. Diana wanted to be treated as an equal and Charles wasn't having it.

I often heard pictures and plates, vases and anything else they could get their hands on being hurled around their apartments along with screams and shouts, but we were instructed to be discreet at all times, so sometimes if I heard a row going on I waited in the corridor till the noise had died down, and only then would I knock.

Very soon after the couple's famous TV interview in 1985, the marriage was effectively over, and Charles stayed at Kensington only infrequently. By 1996 they were divorced. It was Diana's extraordinarily revealing TV interview in 1995 that made the Queen finally intervene. Charles fully accepts his mother's decisions and she determined that the interview had made it impossible for him to do anything other than divorce Diana.

That much earlier interview in 1985 – conducted at Kensington Palace – had opened Pandora's box; Charles and Diana's joint decision to talk about their private lives in front of twenty million people meant that the temptation to talk again, perhaps about less happy days, was always there and Diana's later interviews with the journalist Andrew Morton confirmed that the old royal dogma – never complain, never explain – had been jettisoned. Diana's interviews with Morton seriously damaged Charles's reputation and that of the monarchy. The middle-class virtues of a cosy domestic life with not a mistress in sight – virtues that Queen Victoria had done so much to make a key aspect of the royal family's lives – had come back to bite a man who clearly preferred to live a life akin to that of his Georgian ancestors.

But as the nightmare unfolded, Kensington Palace became a retreat for Diana, perhaps because it had always been more her home rather than Charles's.

A servant who worked at Kensington Palace during these years remembered that:

Diana really loved Kensington. It's where her children were being brought up and where she was happy; it was where she stood up to

Charles. She was conscious that she herself came from one of Britain's noblest families – in many ways, she came from a family that had the edge over the royal family. She liked to point out that Charles was descended from the princes of tiny, usually impoverished, German states; Diana's family had been marrying into the British aristocracy for at least 600 years. They were inextricably linked to all the great families of England, including the Churchills, so it was always unlikely she would simply assume she was lucky to have married Charles whatever the downsides.

After Charles moved permanently out of Kensington Palace in 1992, Diana clearly felt a great sense of relief and release. Kensington was the place where she had her greatest ups and downs: elated one moment, suicidal the next. Nonetheless, through it all she felt hugely supported by her admirers across the world – admirers who, to a large extent, took her side against her erring husband, who seemed awkward and over-entitled when he gave interviews designed to counter Diana's message.

In the five years from 1992 until her death in 1997, Diana's life at Kensington was a curious mix of the serious and sedate and the utterly frivolous – the latter revealing her sometimes eccentric sense of fun and her desire, like a naughty schoolgirl, to shock and amuse others. She loved to throw caution to the wind and behave in ways that she knew were far from what was expected of the Princess of Wales. There was a bit of Diana that disliked the absurd restrictions placed on her and she often broke away in ways that terrified her security staff, or her 'gaolers', as she jokingly referred to them.

Winnifred Watson (not her real name), who worked for Diana at this time, recalled some of the contradictions in her character:

Diana always wanted to combine being a megastar – which is what she was in the last few years of her life – with being a completely anonymous person. In that sense she was just like a pop star or any other celebrity. But, of course, she wasn't just a celebrity – for a time, she was the most famous woman in the world. That fact, as much as anything else, brought out the naughty little girl in her – the one who had not been allowed to be a little girl much as a child, what with boarding school, her parents' divorce and her barking mad stepmother, Raine Spencer.

'What she loved above all at Kensington was to walk round the park while hiding her identity in drab clothes,' recalled one insider.

She'd set off on her own wearing dark glasses and sit on a bench by the Round Pond, just watching passers-by. I think it was a relief from the pressure of life with Charles in the palace, and even after Charles – because in many ways, despite her huge public profile, she wanted to be a private person. The shyness she never lost wasn't fake.

There were several incidents that became the stuff of gossip in the palace – like the time she sat on the end of a park bench by the Round Pond, apparently not noticing that a tramp was snoozing at the other end of the same bench. He hadn't a clue who she was but woke up and started chatting to her; and all credit to her, she wasn't in the least fazed and chatted away quite cheerfully to him. He even offered her a drink from a very suspicious-looking bottle he had in his pocket. She very politely declined, but they talked for about twenty minutes quite happily. He almost certainly hadn't a clue who she was.

I was told by a security officer that on another occasion when she slipped out of the palace without telling anyone, he had set off across the park in pursuit of her and he asked a couple of people if they'd seen a tall young woman in a dark coat. One of them replied that he'd just had a chat with someone fitting the description. She'd petted his dog and had a long chat with him about dogs in general. The man asked who she was and what all the fuss was about. The security officer forgot himself for a moment – he was probably in a panic – and before he could stop himself blurted out, 'The bloody Princess of Wales, that's who!' As he ran off in the direction the dog walker had indicated, the security officer heard just two words from the man: 'Fucking hell!'

On another occasion, she set off into the park one morning and met a group of school children from a local primary school – having been a kindergarten teacher, she was always very good with small children and was soon chatting happily to them and to their teachers. After a while she explained she had to go and it was only then that one teacher said to another, 'Have you any idea who that was? It was the Princess of Wales!'

But the favourite story doing the rounds was that Diana was in the park one day when a large dog began to attack a little terrier – she reacted immediately by taking off one of her shoes and hurling it at the offending dog!

She was supposed to tell her security staff if she wanted to go somewhere, but on many occasions she failed to do this and would set off for the shops in Kensington High Street or for the Round Pond or Serpentine and a few minutes later the security detail would be frantically fanning out across the park looking for her. 'It's my own version of hide and seek,' she would say. But she would always apologise to the security officers later on. Once, she hid behind a hedge that surrounded part of the palace and was approached by one of the park keepers, who told her that the public were not allowed on that side of the hedge. She apologised and walked off. The park keeper apparently had no idea who she was. 'She is very good at making herself look very ordinary,' said one of my colleagues.

One of Diana's favourite places in the palace itself was her small private walled garden, but she also had a rooftop garden that was not always as private as she liked to think. The late 1980s and early 1990s was perhaps the period in which the British were most obsessed with suntans – this was before the risk of skin cancer was fully appreciated. Throughout the summer in those years Diana would sunbathe, often completely naked, on her rooftop.

Occasionally, drowsy from the heat, she would forget herself and stand up, and though it was usually impossible to see anything from the park there was one occasion when a barrier was down and Diana found herself staring at two builders – before she could do anything she saw them both bow deeply and turn away. 'They might have just been builders,' said one of the footmen later on, 'but they were gentlemen all the same.' The bows were so deep that the princess had time to escape before they looked up again.

Helicopters regularly flew over Kensington Palace, of course, but Diana was never bothered and would wave at them, certain they couldn't really see her – until a member of staff gently pointed out that many helicopters are fitted with high-resolution binoculars!

✣

Kensington Palace was the scene of many of Diana's love affairs following the break-up of her marriage. These affairs were not entirely the result of a desire to have revenge upon Charles for his affairs with Camilla and others, but that was certainly part of it. More importantly, while she was involved in an affair she was distracted from the upset of her own past. Affairs were also a distraction from the pressure of her royal life – a life which, even after her divorce, was filled with immensely stressful situations: her love–hate relationship with her celebrity status, and her desire to protect her children from publicity while also recognising her own thirst for publicity.

Winnifred Watson recalled the atmosphere at Kensington Palace at this time:

Old Etonian art dealer Oliver Hoare was one of her first lovers following her divorce and he was famously caught half-naked, hiding behind a potted plant in a corridor at Kensington, but the staff were always seeing half-naked people running around the place. If it wasn't someone or other's lover, it was an elderly relative of the Queen's who had locked him or herself out of the apartment while half in their pyjamas and half out. We were quite used to it and just pretended nothing was amiss or we hadn't seen, though of course we always had – but Diana's efforts to hide what was going on from her staff were pointless. Everyone knew – that was the problem with Kensington Palace. You could not hide anything from anyone – one of the drawbacks of having a large staff and being a member of what was in many ways a nightmare family of dysfunctional people; by that, I mean the royal family. It was something hated by Princess Margaret. Within minutes of arriving at the palace with Tony Armstrong-Jones before she married him – or later on with Roddy Llewellyn or any of her other lovers – the news was all over the palace. Somehow both Margaret and Diana never learned the simple fact that however much you trusted and relied on your staff not to talk about you, talk about you they would. Both Diana and Margaret thought they would be able to hide what was going on, and of course it was impossible.

Diana became seriously obsessed with Oliver Hoare – almost to a deranged extent. She would wander around Kensington in disguise looking for telephone boxes from which she made hundreds of calls to him. Indeed, it got so bad that Hoare's wife suggested they call the police. Diana's frantic calls may have been connected to the fact that Hoare had made her pregnant, but there is no real evidence for this – despite some claims – and the affair eventually petered out. It must have been heartrending for Diana when a small parcel arrived at Kensington Palace – it contained a beautiful pair of her dead father's cufflinks that she had given to Hoare as a present.

The Princess of Wales was always seen as highly sensitive to the needs of children, but most especially her own; so it was no real surprise when, in an interview in May 2019, Prince William confessed that he felt 'pain like no other' when his mother died. But if she was good with children, she was an innocent when it came to meeting politicians and intellectuals. She famously met Israeli premier Shimon Peres, who was discussing the difficult position in the Middle East. Diana said she would 'love to visit Israel – anything for some sun!'

On another occasion she was introduced to a man who told her he was a musician, a harpsichordist. She replied, 'And which instrument do you play?' A cellist who met her on the same occasion at Kensington Palace later said that when she spoke to you:

> You felt that no one else existed. She was absolutely brilliant at making you feel you were the only person of interest to her in the world at that moment. There was none of the usual royal small talk where one is asked, 'And what do you do?', and before you have time to answer they have moved on to the next person.

All of William and Harry's earliest memories are surely tied up with Kensington Palace, although they stayed with the Queen and Prince Charles at Balmoral and Highgrove during holidays from school – even the death of their mother did not dampen the boys' enthusiasm for the palace, for here they had played and enjoyed some of the more normal things never experienced by royal children in previous generations, thanks to Diana. Instead of insisting they learn to shoot pheasants, Diana's outings took them to the McDonald's restaurant in Kensington High Street, for example, and they visited Thorpe Park near Windsor.

When it was time to choose the boys' school, Diana caused some hilarity by saying she was finding it difficult to choose between Eton and the local comprehensive school in Holland Park. One or two officials were horrified when they thought she might even mean it. Either way, the weight of tradition and money prevailed and William was sent to Eton, although he also enjoyed the company of his private tutor – Rory Stewart, later an MP – who had also been at Eton.

If sending her children to a state school was a step too far for Diana, there is no doubt she would have approved of William's decision to propose to Catherine Middleton.

'She would have loved Catherine,' explains Winnifred Watson.

And she would have been very cross that some of the upper-class servants at Kensington – the equerries and so on who hate to think of *themselves* as servants – made cruel jokes about Catherine's mother. They would refer to Catherine's mother as 'Doors to Manual', a reference to her time as an air stewardess.

Mind you, when Diana fell out with Charles and to some extent with the whole of 'the Firm', as she famously used to call the royal family, she wasn't averse to making naughty jokes about them. She used to joke that all of Charles's problems were genetic; that he was the result of too much in-breeding between 'big-nosed German midgets'. Don't be fooled – Diana could be very cutting if she felt someone deserved it!

There is no doubt that the British royal family has survived, while most European monarchies have vanished, because they are adaptable – it wasn't just advances in the study of genetics that made them realise that constantly marrying their relatives was a bad thing. The need to seem less detached from ordinary life allowed the marriage of William and Catherine, a union that would have been inconceivable in Tommy Lascelles's day, or even as recently as the 1970s. Among the upper-class servants who attend the Queen and the Duke of Edinburgh there were still strenuous behind-the-scenes efforts to stop the marriage between William and Catherine – it was only William's insistence, and his memory of his mother's desire that her sons should marry for love and not for dynastic reasons, that eventually made William's marriage possible. If the old guard had had its way, William's life might have been marred just as his great-aunt Margaret's life was. Today's equivalents of Tommy Lascelles have not changed as much as we might like to believe – drawn from the same grand circles from which they always came, they are invariably a generation or two out of touch. Even the Queen was apparently surprised by their resistance to the idea of William and Catherine's marriage – she, on the other hand, pragmatic to the last and concerned above all for the long-term survival of the royal family, knew that allowing the marriage was shrewd and strategic.

But if the grandees were concerned that William planned to marry a commoner, they were apoplectic when Prince Harry explained his desire to marry Meghan Markle, a divorced mixed-race American. Meghan would almost certainly have been prevented from marrying Harry but for the risk that Harry might break away and marry her anyway – rather like his ancestor the Duke of Sussex did many years before. Invoking the Royal Marriages Act to try to prevent Harry and Meghan marrying might well have led to irreparable damage to the royal family's reputation. Of course, the other side of it is that Harry and Meghan were always less vulnerable to pressure from 'tweedy types' – simply because neither Harry nor his offspring will ever sit on the throne.

CHAPTER SIXTEEN

BOYS' NIGHT OUT

'Everyone likes flattery; and when you come to royalty,
you should lay it on with a trowel.'

BENJAMIN DISRAELI

As Prince Harry reached his late teens, he was occasionally photographed stumbling out of Fulham nightclubs or into Kensington Palace in the early hours, clearly the worse for drink. The press made much of this, but most people completely understood that this was normal adolescent behaviour and it could be easily forgiven in a teenager whose mother had died when he was still too young to fully comprehend what that meant.

But wherever he went Harry always returned, as his brother did, to the palace that had been his main home for as long as he could remember.

One of Harry's closest friends confirmed that 'he always saw Kensington Palace as a sort of sanctuary, because the idea of the palace was inseparable from the idea of his mother'.

Like his brother, Harry also sought to escape some of the traditions foisted on the sons of royalty, but neither escaped that curious tradition that many have seen as vaguely inappropriate in the twenty-first century – military training.

Writing in the *Daily Express*, the journalist Stephen Bygrave explained:

One might almost think a military career is seen as important in the royal family just in case these young men might need to lead an army into battle on horseback as their ancestors did six hundred years ago. It's all down to an ancient idea that the profession of arms is the most noble of professions. But the whole thing is a nonsense because although young royal males are exposed to risks, those risks are always controlled in ways they are not controlled for regular soldiers and airmen.

But it is perhaps absurd to expect the children of what is, after all, the ultimate celebrity family to lead ordinary lives, as an anonymous *Times* journalist explained:

We don't want the royals to lead real lives – when Harry was accused of cheating, or getting a little too much help with his A levels to ensure he got into Sandhurst, we should not have been surprised or offended. It was just part of a long tradition – Harry's father was admitted to Cambridge with A level grades that would have ensured an instant rejection for any other applicant. His great-great-great-grandfather Edward VII, who famously owned more horses than books, was admitted to both Oxford and Cambridge. The sons of royalty don't have to be good at anything, they just have to be. Harry's grandmother made him Duke of

Sussex, Earl of Dumbarton and Baron Kilkeel. No one seriously thinks these honours were *deserved*.

But if negotiating a few years in the military was perfectly manageable for Harry and William, negotiating the relationship between themselves and their wives was to prove far more difficult and it led to rifts between the brothers that will take many years to heal.

Meanwhile at Kensington, squabbles continued between the various older residents who no doubt hoped they could live quietly and luxuriously without anyone noticing – among those who lived at the palace both before and during the period when Harry and William were growing up were the Duke and Duchess of Gloucester, Prince Michael of Kent and his wife Marie-Christine (known rather unkindly by the press as 'Princess Pushy'). Prince Michael's elder brother, Prince Edward, the Duke of Kent also lives at the palace with *his* wife Katharine. Princess Alice, Duchess of Gloucester lived at the palace until her death aged 102 in 2004. Typical of the older generation, she would have her servants issue a notice to other residents if she was planning to go out. The idea was that if everyone else knew then no one would dare upstage her by leaving at the same time or just before. One hilarious notice, quoted by Andrew Morton, read, 'At 11.15 the Duchess of Gloucester will depart Kensington Palace for a hair appointment.'

Some of the older residents seem to have flown under the press's radar, but Prince and Princess Michael of Kent were not so lucky: the newspapers had a field day when it was discovered in the early

2000s they were living virtually rent-free in their huge apartment at Kensington.

They eventually agreed to pay market rent, but the row left a bad taste and was an additional reminder to the minor royals especially that the days of deference are well and truly over.

The difficulty for the less prominent Kensington residents is that they cannot help feeling they work hard for their privileges and they are baffled when the outside world does not value them as they value themselves.

Less criticism has been directed at Prince William as he will eventually be king, and few would dispute the fact that the job of monarch is an onerous one. He and Catherine have still caused controversy, however. Just as we have seen with virtually every other incoming Kensington resident, William and Kate simply refused to manage with the apartments they inherited. Changes just had to be made. In their case, the so-called need for refurbishment and reordering has been taken to extraordinary lengths. The staff of Historic Royal Palaces is to be moved from the main palace into a huge subterranean basement being built under the grounds of the palace garden and under the Orangery. This will then allow the royal couple's teams of nannies, footmen, maids, secretaries, and press and communications experts to move into the vacated area.

Of course, this extravagance is to some extent the fault of an inquisitive public – the more we want to know about William and Kate, the more the royal family feels the need to manage and perfect its public persona.

John Regan (not his real name), who worked in the communications department at Kensington, explained that both William and Harry often joke about the absurd position they find themselves in. They were particularly bemused by the jargon used by the teams of public relations people foisted upon them.

> The standing joke at Kensington Palace is that everyone knows that press and public relations teams are bound to make any situation worse when a crisis arises. Members of the royal family, like everyone else, feel they have to employ these people but half the time they don't trust them – the other half, they don't even know what they are talking about! I remember we all laughed when we saw the CV of one PR 'professional' who got a job helping to manage Harry's public persona. Apparently, he had – and I quote – 'overseen global corporate accounts with a particular emphasis on thought leadership and purpose-led campaigns'. When Prince Harry saw that he said, 'What the fuck does that mean?'

The royal family's relationship with the media has always been fraught – since the early eighteenth century when the Prince Regent was mercilessly lampooned, often in the most grotesque manner, the press has known that it is always open season on members of the royal family. One might argue that the increase in criticism and the feeling that the public had a right to appraise the royals was in exact inverse proportion to the monarchy's loss of power. Before the Glorious Revolution of 1688, anyone seriously lampooning a member of the royal family would be very likely to find himself having his nose or ears cut off. And in the Prince Regent's day, the writer Leigh Hunt was sent to prison for two years for describing the prince as 'a fat Adonis of fifty'. It is not difficult to imagine that most of Kensington Palace's residents would welcome a return to more deferential days.

Once imprisonment as a punishment for insulting a royal was no longer allowed, the floodgates opened, and they were opened further in more recent times by the Princess of Wales's understandable desire to get the media on her side in her battle with Prince Charles.

Each new generation of royals thinks it can control how the media portrays them, but the media is like fire – play with it and eventually you will get your fingers burned. In trying to portray himself as a concerned environmentalist, for example, Charles has been mocked for talking to plants. According to a former Highgrove gardener, Charles would walk around his garden admonishing some plants and comforting others. 'I heard him say to a jasmine, "Now look, the last time we spoke I was gentle and encouraging, but you haven't come on a bit since then. I'm going to have to be firmer with you. That may seem harsh but it's for your own good."'

The Sun regularly reports that Charles makes a point of 'shaking hands' with every tree he helps to plant, at the same time wishing it well. This kind of thing may make Charles a laughing stock in some quarters, but many others rather like and admire his New Age eccentricities.

Since William's marriage and the birth of his three children, Kensington has become a hive of public relations effort; as the couple's public relations machine grew, older royal residents looked on, knowing from their own experience that the younger royals would have to go through difficult times, as John Regan explains:

When Princess Margaret lived at Kensington along with Princess Alice, the Kents and even the dreaded Tommy Lascelles, there were always rows and tensions – Margaret would literally spit on the ground if she caught sight of Lascelles across one of the palace courtyards – and because none of the royal residents were, in reality, as important as members of the immediate family, they were forever squabbling over precedence, but they hated the idea that anyone outside the palace would find out about this. If Margaret was planning to go out, she expected her staff to let other residents know they were not to leave before she did. The other families were just as bad as they insisted on their place in the pecking order.

But everything changed when Diana came to Kensington Palace. She did as she pleased when she pleased because of course she could – she was the Princess of Wales and the most important resident apart from her husband. The other residents were either jealous of her or infuriated by what they saw as her refusal to obey the rules *they* had obeyed for decades.

When the adult William arrived with his family of course it was expected that the arrogant young royals would overreach themselves. By this time, they knew that it was best to keep your head down and not try to control the press – everyone eventually acknowledges that the Queen's motto, 'never complain, never explain' is best. But they all believed the younger royals, with their new children and over-confident outlook, would not heed this advice.

This has certainly proved to be the case, especially when William and Kate were joined by Harry and Meghan. At first the two couples got on well – William and Harry had always been close – but inevitably there were tensions, as one insider explains:

> Both William and Harry were always likely to be drawn to confident, strong women because they lost their mother so early. Kate is actually one of the nicest royals and she hasn't let life in her extremely grand apartment at Kensington go to her head – or at least not too much. She is nice to her staff, in the main, and she was very warm towards Meghan when she arrived. But tensions were bound to arise because Meghan inevitably had to accept that although she is a duchess she is not married to the next king. I think she has found that difficult to deal with and although Harry loved their cottage in the grounds of Kensington Palace, Meghan was conscious that it was tiny in comparison to the vast apartment complex where Kate and William live. Harry has nothing to prove. Meghan has everything to prove. That's the problem.
>
> I know, for example, that tensions reached such a pitch that the Queen herself was driven to Kensington from Buckingham Palace to try to stop the bickering.

But perhaps it is unfair to expect William and Harry's wives to become friends. 'I agree,' says a former member of staff:

> It is unfair, especially in the hothouse atmosphere at Kensington, where older royals resent the new arrivals because the new arrivals are more glamorous and have more power within the family. The two couples – I mean Harry and Meghan, and William and Kate – did get on initially but didn't actually see much of each other, despite living in close proximity, but being a royal goes to everyone's head eventually and after

a while William and Harry would meet without their wives in tow to avoid rows and stony silences.

If power corrupts, and absolute power corrupts absolutely, the best example is perhaps found at Kensington Palace. Harry, William and Kate – and to a lesser extent Meghan – are treated with ridiculous levels of deference within the palace, so it's said that they are always furious and baffled when the media and others outside the hothouse don't treat them in the same way. As one irreverent member of staff put it:

> They forget they just happen to have been lucky – they came out of the right vagina! It's almost as if the very walls of the palace have a baleful influence on the inhabitants – going right back to Princess Margaret and earlier, everyone who lives at the palace eventually becomes jealous and suspicious – sometimes even paranoid – about what everyone else is thinking and doing.

According to one report in the satirical magazine *Private Eye*:

> The rivalry between Meghan and Kate is very real. Kate remains semi-detached from it all, secure in her position as a future queen, and wife and mother of kings, with nothing to prove. But her sister-in-law now realises she will never again have the largest star on her dressing room door and that her role on the royal stage will only get smaller.

The panic this induced was palpable at Kensington Palace and explains why Harry and Meghan moved to Frogmore Cottage in the grounds of Windsor Castle. They had been due to move into the apartment next to William and Kate's – an apartment vacated by the Duke and Duchess of Gloucester precisely for that reason and then refurbished (again) for Harry and Meghan. Now that apartment remains empty and unused, an expensive taxpayer-funded embarrassment that the royal family would rather keep quiet about. The move to Windsor was no doubt partly down to Meghan and Harry having a child, but also due to a desire for lives outside the shadow of more important royals. Living next door to William and Kate was perhaps a step too far for Meghan. And as with every other royal who has ever moved into a royal apartment at Kensington or any other palace, Harry and Meghan's move to Frogmore led to the usual demand that their accommodation was simply unacceptable without major refurbishment. The taxpayer cost of refurbishing Frogmore Cottage for Harry and Meghan was two and a half million pounds.

That Meghan was in charge of the work and that she is the dominating figure in their lives generally was revealed when Harry admitted that 'what Meghan wants, Meghan gets'. This particular statement referred to the couple's wedding arrangements, but it is hard to believe that Meghan would be this focused and determined solely in the run-up to the wedding, and not equally so when it came to the rest of their lives.

But this cuts no ice with the staff at Kensington, who according to reliable reports began using rather unflattering nicknames for Meghan within weeks of her arrival: she is 'Me-Gain', or the 'Duchess of Difficult' or even 'Di 2' or 'Di Lite', a cruel reference to what some have seen as her desire to outshine Diana, Princess of Wales.

Royal courtiers at Kensington – the same tweedy, British, public school, ex-army aristocrats they have always been – simply did not know what to make of Meghan. After receiving a number of severe reprimands from her they were apparently relieved when she moved to Windsor, but this relief was tempered by deep anxiety at what she might do next. As we will see in the final chapter of this book, such anxiety was completely justified. When Edward Lane Fox, Harry's private secretary, resigned in 2018, the feeling was that Meghan planned to do her own PR – always a high-risk strategy, but 'at least it will all happen some distance from Kensington Palace and the heir to the throne,' as one former royal public relations man put it.

Some of the potential pitfalls of Meghan trying to control what is written about her and her husband were revealed when the couple denounced social media, only to then set up their own Instagram account. They had pointedly chosen not to share the Kensington Palace account – the result of having their own account was not that Meghan and Harry were suddenly able to wander peacefully along the sunlit digital uplands, but rather that they were faced with a barrage of unpleasant and sometimes downright racist messages.

Back at Kensington Palace, the courtiers are running hither and thither not knowing quite what to do – having dealt only with royals and aristocrats who share the same or very similar backgrounds, they long for the old days when someone like Meghan would not have had a chance of marrying into the royal family.

As another former palace employee put it:

The old, rather grand courtiers, often descended from long lines of courtiers, live on their country estates when not advising the royals and their attitudes are basically either eighteenth century or a mix of eighteenth century and 1950s. They wish they could do to Meghan what they did to Princess Margaret in the 1950s and 1960s. But if Margaret were alive, she might well be cheering Meghan on for doing what she was never able to do. She was always a rebel and Meghan is too – although she very cleverly ingratiates herself with Prince Charles and with the Queen who adores her. The Queen has a soft spot for Americans after meeting Barack Obama who she completely fell in love with – so much so that she has frequently asked her courtiers if they could arrange for him to come to Britain now he is no longer President.

Meanwhile, Meghan and Harry used personal friends associated with their favourite members' club, Soho House, to try to get their message across – something that once again fills the old guard with horror but helps Meghan feel she is an independent presence, not one that is subsumed by the William and Kate publicity machine.

A former member of the Kensington Palace public relations team said:

Meghan approaches all this as if she were still an actress. And, of course, being part of the British royal family does involve something very much akin to acting. She is not going to let others tell her what sort of part to play – she wants to interpret the role as she sees fit and she worries that people will look down on her or treat her differently because she is a divorced, mixed-race American. And there are the more reactionary elements in the royal family who do look down on her and she knows it. This makes her overreact sometimes – she doesn't have Kate's assured way of dealing with people. Famously, Kate was horrified when Meghan shouted at a member of Kate's staff – that was definitely the beginning of discussions about leaving Kensington Palace. And like many people not used to dealing with servants, Meghan overdoes the imperiousness;

so on the one hand she wants to be like Diana, a people's princess, and on the other she wants people to stand to attention when she clicks her fingers.

Since Harry and Meghan's departure, you will notice that communications from Frogmore tend to involve Harry and Meghan exclusively – pictures of the royal couple tend to be carefully cropped to remove William and Kate before being uploaded to Instagram. It's sad but perhaps inevitable and what the palace doesn't understand is that the more they deny that there is a rift, the less people will believe them. As the old adage has it – journalists can be relied on to make things up 90 per cent of the time, but press officers and communications people can be relied on to make things up 100 per cent of the time!

❧

The tragedy for everyone living at Kensington Palace in the modern era is that they must survive an intrusive, often unsympathetic media while being hugely sensitive to accusations that, in an aspiring meritocracy, they have done nothing to deserve their elevated status. They want to be portrayed positively, but they also want it to be on their own terms; they long more than anything for positive publicity while insisting on their right to privacy – a right that many would question given the royal family's drain on the public purse.

The split between the way Meghan wants to run things and the way the old guard like to do it can best be seen in the farce that followed the birth of Harry and Meghan's son Archie in 2019. The Buckingham Palace press office insisted they would be the ones to issue a press release following the birth, but Meghan and Harry had other ideas, proceeding to announce it on their Instagram account without telling the palace.

Having been upstaged, Buckingham Palace retreated into old-style pomposity. They issued an absurdly grand press release stating that 'the Queen, the Duke of Edinburgh, the Duke and Duchess of Cambridge, Lady Jane Fellowes, Lady Sara McCorquodale and Earl Spencer have been informed and are delighted with the news. The Duchess's mother, Doria Ragland, who is overjoyed by the arrival of her first grandchild, is with Their Royal Highnesses at Frogmore Cottage.' A glaring omission was that Meghan's father was not mentioned.

This is just the kind of thing that Meghan was trying to escape, but the perils of escape are legion, as Ron Wilson explained:

What Meghan and even Kate don't realise is that after the first flush of excitement, being part of the royal family is a life sentence – during which you must develop a very thick skin or go under. Rather than ignoring the older members of the royal family who still live at Kensington, the younger royals should try to learn from them. They have in many cases weathered the media attacks and mockeries; they've accepted that they must be careful with both their behaviour and their public announcements or the hoi polloi (a favourite phrase of the old guard!) might once again begin asking, as Willie Hamilton once asked, 'What are they for? Why are we paying for them?'

And if it is hard for the younger royals, it is easy to imagine how much harder it is for their staff at Kensington.

In the modern era, many members of staff have been sacked for being too friendly or over-familiar. Even modern, 'ordinary' royals like

Meghan and Kate hate their staff to get above themselves – which is why, for example, protection officers have in the past been 'removed' for the tiniest breaches of protocol. As a journalist writing for *Private Eye* explained, staff have been sacked or moved 'on the grounds that a royal disliked their aftershave, found an unsightly mole offensive or objected to the wearing of ties that weren't silk. One was shifted from his job for offering a sweet to a child princess in front of a parent. Friendliness is never permitted.'

A casual observer from the late seventeenth century would certainly recognise Kensington Palace today. The state rooms and the external appearance are much as they were left by Christopher Wren and William Kent. Internally, of course, the rest of the vast palace would be largely unrecognisable after an endless series of scrapings and alterations.

Yet the atmosphere of the palace – the human atmosphere – even beyond the state rooms echoes curiously from earlier epochs. The inhabitants of the palace are much as the inhabitants have always been: intoxicated, to a greater or lesser degree, by their extraordinarily elevated status; fearful of criticism and desperate for praise; obsessed with, and to some extent embarrassed by, the social divisions between lower staff, grand staff and residents. These distinctions, though superficially eased, are ultimately as rigid as they were centuries ago. In the wider world outside the palace, the royals must try to be all things to all men – stars in the royal firmament, yet in possession of the common touch (though the word 'common' must never be used!).

In a sense, Kensington Palace, the bricks and mortar symbol of royalty, and the flesh and blood royals themselves have both been transformed into a single entity in the eyes of the worldwide public. They are the architectural and human aspects of one great historical yearning for heritage.

※

Kensington Palace is an odd sort of hybrid. Much of it is as modern as a Barratt home in Surrey, despite the external walls giving an impression of earlier centuries. Only the grand state rooms, which were once the heart of the English court, remain much as they were 300 years ago.

There have always been complaints that the royal family hands out grace-and-favour apartments to relatives who really do very little to deserve grand accommodation in a beautiful park in central London, but cousins and second cousins of the Queen, elderly nieces and members of the aristocracy who were courtiers in their youth will always find a home in a palace that is actually much bigger than it may seem to visitors restricted to the state rooms.

Perhaps we don't really mind, since our love affair with the royal family has usually extended to grumbling while continuing to fund them. There is no doubt that were it not for the British fondness for the past, the royal family might well have gone the way of most other European royal families. There is no doubt, too, that public sympathy has always been sufficient to keep afloat an institution that provides the rest of us with a fantasy life. If they are wise, the royals will not try too hard to modernise; overdo it and they will lose the very traditionalism that has ensured their survival. We may laugh at the absurdity of toddlers being made dukes, and moving with the seasons between grand houses in different parts of the country; we may laugh at the royals' addiction to stalking deer and shooting pheasants; but at some deep level we would love to be part of the same world.

It has been said that every little girl wishes to be a princess. In the past it was impossible, but now, tempting us into continual approval, we have seen it happen – for Catherine Middleton, the daughter of a company director from Berkshire, and for Meghan Markle, the descendant of black American slaves.

It is as if, just as Queen Victoria knew she could get the public on her side by opening Kensington Palace to the public, so too has Queen Elizabeth II understood that to keep public favour today, the magic dust of royalty needed to be sprinkled a little more widely; that the royal family could no longer afford to continue the ancient practice of marrying the remnants of vanishing European royal houses, and instead needed to embrace, to some degree, the increasing egalitarianism of the twenty-first century.

And if it is all just a fairy tale made real, then a fairy tale needs a suitable setting. And what better setting than the great palace of varieties at Kensington?

POSTSCRIPT

'One kisses, one allows the kiss.'

Since the publication of the first edition of this book, the long saga of the royals at Kensington Palace has carried on as two of the palace's most famous recent residents – Meghan Markle and Prince Harry – have continued to struggle to find their place in the world. Or perhaps, more accurately, their palace in the world.

Their moves from Kensington Palace to Windsor, then to Canada and then to a vast mansion in Montecito, California, speak volumes about a couple who have yet to realise that living in a particular place is not necessarily going to make you happy.

Having furiously denied that leaving Kensington had anything to do with a family rift – a huge row, in fact, between Harry and his brother William – the couple departed for Windsor and Frogmore Cottage, despite the fact that they were already living in a delightful house in the grounds of Kensington Palace and despite the fact that a magnificent twenty-room apartment was being prepared for them in the palace itself.

A rather lovely late Georgian house (*not* a cottage), Frogmore sits quietly in the gloom of Windsor Great Park well away from prying eyes and passing vehicles. It must have seemed the perfect retreat from what Meghan and Harry saw as an unsympathetic, unfair world of media speculation and criticism; a world in which William and Kate took centre stage. But as Meghan and Harry quickly discovered, their flight to Windsor did not mean an escape from the world's enquiring eye; instead, it revealed to that world a lack of foresight.

Many of us know people who, desperate to escape the pressures of city life, sell up and move to some remote spot in the countryside only to find the loneliness and isolation far more difficult to cope with than the demands of life in the metropolis. Most of us don't have enough money to indulge the whims of this kind of fantasy. Having left Kensington, Meghan and Harry quickly found that away from the lights and noise of central London, in the quiet acres of Windsor Park with the mist rolling up through the dark trees from the river, they were still unhappy. One insider claims that having overseen the renovation of Frogmore Cottage, 'Meghan realised that living there would be like living in the Russian steppe'. Its remoteness made Kensington seem like the centre of the universe. That was the final straw. 'I don't want to retire to rural obscurity,' she is said to have complained.

It was so obvious to most commentators – including someone who had previously worked for Meghan and Harry – that this is exactly what would happen. Trying to escape the noise and bustle leads to a new discovery: that living without noise and bustle can be worse.

By the time the royal couple realised what life at Frogmore would really be like, a fortune had been spent 'renovating' the house (or making it look like a Californian condo, as one builder put it to me).

Frogmore Cottage is considerably bigger than Meghan and Harry's former home at Kensington Palace. Here they lived in Nottingham Cottage, a beautiful house which retains at least some of the features originally installed by Sir Christopher Wren. It was, and is, cosy, wonderfully private and yet within a minute's walk of Kensington High Street, ten minutes from the grand shops of Sloane Street and Park Lane and a short drive from the Queen at Buckingham Palace. As we go to press, speculation is rife that Princess Beatrice and her husband Edoardo Mapelli Mozzi will soon be living at Nottingham Cottage. They will be neighbours of Beatrice's sister Princess Eugenie and her husband Jack Brooksbank, who are already living in Ivy Cottage. Eugenie, Beatrice and their partners are likely to lead far quieter lives at Kensington than Meghan and Harry, whose rift with Kate and William was deep enough to begin the series of moves that led eventually to California – it's reported that by the spring of 2019, the two couples were not even on speaking terms.

The search for an ideal place to live is symptomatic of a profound difference between Meghan and Harry; a difference that lies dormant while love and passion have the upper hand.

Born into the royal family, Harry has never known anything outside the royal bubble; he is not ambitious or driven, for there was never a need for either of these qualities. He has the laid-back, diffident attitude of all senior royal males who have always accepted as their due the deference and respect of those around them. Having lived inside the bubble for so long, Harry thinks that life outside will be a breath of freedom and fresh air, but, as his great-great-uncle Edward VIII discovered after abdicating, the grass for members of the royal family is not always greener on the other side. Harry has been famous from birth. He does not have to struggle to find his place in the world because it has been given to him and he has been trained from birth to accept it.

Meghan, on the other hand, was not born famous or especially privileged; her fierce ambition, combined with startling good looks and some acting ability, led to a reasonably successful career in television. When she met Harry, her drive and ambition – and the fact that, according to insiders, she made all the running – entranced a young man who by nature and upbringing was waiting to be led. It is not true to say that he is a weak character, though some have claimed this; it is more that, like many men who lose their mothers early in life, he is drawn to strong women. He is not leadership material; Meghan is.

After the initial glamour of being a senior royal in London wore off, according to her friends, Meghan was horrified at the thought that she might spend the rest of her life being driven from Kensington Palace to various official functions; to charity luncheons; to hospital opening ceremonies; to dreary summers at Balmoral and Christmases at Sandringham.

This prospect appalled her. She saw it as a kind of prison. Several of Harry's former girlfriends are known to have been careful to avoid reaching the point in the relationship at which marriage and imprisonment within the royal family became a probability, or in some cases even a possibility. They knew that, though gilded, the cage they were being offered was just that – a cage. Coming from America, Meghan saw only the gilding; she failed to spot the cage until it was too late.

In *An African Journey*, the documentary covering the couple's 2019 tour of Africa, Meghan herself admitted that she was 'naïve' about the implications of joining the royal family and facing the British tabloids, despite warnings from British friends. And it is certainly true that the British press, especially the tabloids, treated her in ways that must often have seemed baffling – one minute flattering, the next vindictive and even cruel. The difficulty is that there is no legal definition of what is fair or unfair, and much of the reporting about Meghan was actually just opinion – and opinion has little to do with fairness.

But for a woman of Meghan's self-assurance the solution was straightforward. Her controversial suggestion was that she and Harry would be working royals for part of the year and live in America and do other – more commercial – things for the rest of the year.

Completely misjudging how the royal family works as an institution, Meghan was astonished to find that she and Harry would have to make a decision to be either fully in or fully out; they had to be full-time working royals or, effectively, ex-royals. Part-time royalty at taxpayers' expense was not an option.

According to a former PR specialist at Kensington Palace, Meghan was also baffled and furious when the Queen vetoed the idea that the couple could set up a business in Canada under the name Sussex Royal. For Meghan, the royal family is simply a brand, and as a member of the family, she believes the brand is hers to use as she sees fit. However, the royal family is not just a brand, and the British establishment's traditional proprieties were always going to conflict with Meghan's belief that she can have all the benefits of being a member of the royal family with none of the disadvantages.

There are historical precedents for this vast failure to understand how the royal family works. The Queen loves Americans and America – she famously adores the Obamas – but deep in her psyche lies the memory of her uncle David, later Edward VIII, and, fairly or not, she retains a profound sense that an American, in the shape of Mrs Simpson, led Edward VIII away from his duty into a fantasy existence which turned out to be a lonely, useless life of increasingly bitter exile. She does not want Harry to find himself a lost soul in the same way.

And no intelligent commentator can have failed to notice that all the talk of moves from Kensington to Canada, from Canada to Los Angeles – it all centres on Meghan and not Harry. And do Harry and Meghan share the same views on everything from social justice and racism to the Sussex Royal brand? However much we try to disguise the fact, it is clear that Meghan runs the show. Harry admitted as much when he said that 'what Meghan wants, Meghan gets'.

When Meghan and Harry fell out with William and Kate and the whole royal machine, sources close to the Queen were heard mumbling about the deep significance of Harry's off-the-cuff phrase; the burden of what they were saying was that if Meghan, like Mrs Simpson, gets what she wants, then look out. 'We mustn't forget history in case we are condemned to repeat it,' said one.

It is clear that Meghan's greatest difficulty in the UK is the press. She prefers the more deferential media in her home country, who do not have the complex relationship with the royal family and their partners that the British media do. This is a major reason for the move back to the United States. But we should remember that the press in the UK

has always adored Harry – the newspapers might have done some mor-
alising in the days when he fell rather than walked out of nightclubs,
but there is something innocent and unassuming about him that leads
to mostly positive coverage, not to mention the deep underlying sympathy, even among hard-bitten hacks, for a man whose mother died in
terrible circumstances when he was only twelve. A palace insider was
once quoted as saying about Harry: 'The first strong-willed girl who
comes along will make mincemeat of him.'

The British press and especially the tabloid press has not been so
kind to Meghan. Even her worst enemy would agree that much of the
coverage of Meghan has been unpleasant and unnecessary, and it might
be argued that the newspapers would have sold just as well if they'd
continually sung Meghan's praises. But the true test of character and
fitness to be part of the royal family is whether or not you can put up
with criticism, however unfair it may seem. A former editor of *Private
Eye* once said that if you sue when someone writes something nasty
about you, the story never goes away; old errors and long-forgotten
mistakes are dredged up to blacken your character; the legal case and
the behaviour that gave rise to it are discussed endlessly as the lawyers
battle it out. If, on the other hand, you ignore the story, it is forgotten
within days. It seems that Harry and Meghan have overlooked the fact
that the aim of the press and the media is always to get two bites of the
cherry: first, the celebrity (royal or otherwise) is lauded and praised,
then when the press runs out of material, the process of criticism and
sometimes condemnation begins.

In this respect one has to take one's hat off to Charles and Camilla.
Whatever else one might say about the couple, they have put up with
hurtful criticism for several decades and though they have sometimes

complained they have never sued. The result is that they are generally admired by traditional supporters of the royal family and earlier criticisms have been forgotten. The key thing to remember is that news is ephemeral – here today and forgotten tomorrow – unless you give it the oxygen of publicity.

When Meghan and Harry moved to the United States it was to what has been described as their dream family home. They have a Californian mansion that covers 18,000 square feet. 'Just enough for two adults and a baby,' as one insider put it. The house includes nine bedrooms and sixteen bathrooms. They have celebrities for neighbours – Orlando Bloom and Katy Perry among others – and Meghan at least will feel she is safe among equals; among people who understand her and will give her space.

According to a friend who asked not to be named, the reason the couple bought the house in Montecito centred on the fact that it has a gym, a cinema, a games room, a sauna, a library, a children's cottage in the 5.4-acre grounds for Archie, a tennis court and a swimming pool. In other words, it has enough to keep Harry occupied and reduces the need for him to risk his security by going outside.

The size of the Montecito house might also be interpreted as Meghan and Harry putting two fingers up to the royal family. At Kensington, trips outside the palace had to be made with security staff and this hardly lessened the couple's sense that they were imprisoned; in California, their house is so big that they can have far more freedom than was ever possible at Kensington or Frogmore and without much of a security risk. But if Kensington was a gilded cage, Montecito is too – it's just much bigger. Harry still can't leave the grounds alone without security.

Veteran royal photographer Arthur Edwards, who has always been popular with the royal family, has publicly stated that he feels Harry is unhappy. Edwards says you can see this whenever Harry appears in front of the cameras. Some may agree; others will disagree, but few can dispute that Harry showed no interest in leaving the royal family before his marriage. No doubt the compromise he sought – being a part-time royal – was seen as a way to avoid hurting the Queen while keeping Meghan happy. He was clearly upset that this idea was rejected by the Queen. Arthur Edwards's claim that Harry has looked miserable ever since Meghan appeared on the scene may be going too far, but her search for happiness has certainly created turmoil.

In the very act of escaping the pressures of being a full-time royal based at Kensington Palace, Harry embraced a new set of pressures, primarily the stress of knowing that his grandmother – his commander-in-chief, as he puts it – was not prepared to agree to what he and Meghan saw as a compromise between their desire to be working royals and their wish to live independently of the royal family.

❧

We don't have to go as far as one American 'foot expert', who claimed that because Meghan's second toe is longer than her big toe, she wants to dominate and control; that really would be unfair. But few would dispute that Meghan is a powerful, determined personality, and in any successful couple, if one leads then the other must follow.

Perhaps being mocked for applying porridge and turmeric to her face would upset Meghan, but many of us would say that mockery of such beauty treatments is entirely fair and reasonable. Or if we poked fun at the fact that, having only lived in London for a few months, Meghan decided to publish something on her blog called 'The insider's guide to London'.

And even Meghan might have to admit that it was an error of judgement to announce, before consulting the Queen, that she and Harry were no longer going to be full-time working royals. Likewise, criticising the Queen for stripping Harry of his military appointments was bound to get Meghan into hot water. Allegedly, at the time, Meghan said, 'The powers [of the monarchy] are, unfortunately, greater than me.'

The couple's spat with the royal family was far more serious than we were perhaps led to believe in the early part of 2019. But those subtle signals were always there – the Queen's 2019 Christmas message included a photograph of the Cambridges in the background, with no sign of Meghan and Harry, for instance.

Sharp-eyed royal watchers spotted a possible riposte in Meghan's September 2020 broadcast from her home in which a picture that included the line 'I love you, California' was clearly visible behind her.

And if Meghan really is the driving force behind the couple's move first to Frogmore, then Canada and finally California, it might be that the world is not entirely blind; it may be that the world is actually rather good at interpreting the subtle and not-so-subtle clues in a manner that is entirely reasonable.

Meghan and Harry would do much better to learn from the Queen, who is widely admired for her policy of 'never complain, never explain', and accept that the best way to stop the papers writing unkind things is simply not to fret over it when they do. Just wait for them to get bored and move on. It has worked wonderfully well for the Queen for more than half a century.

But the couple have, in a sense, had the fair coverage they long for. The book *Finding Freedom* – which Meghan and Harry insist they had no hand in – shows them in a golden, uncritical light.

The couple's desire to earn their own living might seem laudable and their £112 million deal with the film-streaming company Netflix shows that even without the Sussex Royal brand they are rapidly heading towards being, well, a brand. It also shows that Meghan and Harry are tough negotiators – Netflix boss Reed Hastings explained that the couple had offered themselves to all the big companies before agreeing their Netflix deal.

But as Arthur Edwards has argued, however much Meghan may enjoy such things, Harry will hate appearing on Oprah Winfrey and other TV chat shows; he will hate trying to do voiceovers for various worthy films. He is not a natural performer. Are we really being asked to believe that he pushed hard for that deal with Netflix? Does he really want to be in showbiz, or does the couple's move in that direction have far more to do with Meghan getting what Meghan wants?

Left to his own devices, would Harry really have announced that he wanted to make documentaries that 'inform but also give hope'? The phrase has a sanctimonious air quite alien to what we know of Harry's character.

While some royals have benefited from planned TV appearances (like Diana, boosting her profile as the People's Princess in her famous interview with Martin Bashir, or walking through minefields in Angola to campaign against the use of landmines – thus cementing her image as a compassionate humanitarian), others haven't fared so well. Andrew's attempt to 'put the record straight' over his relationship with the convicted sex offender Jeffrey Epstein ended in disaster. Meghan and Harry were surely unwise to turn a television programme about some of the poorest people in the world (*An African Journey*) into what some saw as a lament about their own circumstances and how badly they had been treated. Much of the press inevitably reacted by drawing attention to the couple's private jets, luxurious lifestyle and the millions of pounds spent refurbishing a cottage for their use at Windsor. It remains to be seen whether their work with Netflix will be more successful in highlighting the causes they are passionate about.

Meghan and Harry suffer acutely from a problem that afflicts all wealthy people who wish to do good. They are always in danger of being criticised for giving advice to the world's poorest and most disadvantaged from a position of great wealth and privilege. However you dress it up, it does not look good – ever. Criticism from across the world would no doubt cease if Meghan announced that the fortune she shares with her husband meant that they were able to work full-time and unpaid for a number of charities here and in the United States.

But whether the couple will move again, whether the marriage will last, whether their critics are wrong, only time will tell, and we would do well to remember that the only prediction about the future that can be relied on is that all predictions about the future are liable to be wrong. Some royal couples survive the pressures of the press and the royal establishment, while for others, perhaps most famously Princess Margaret and Peter Townsend, it is all too much and the result is the end of the relationship.

A former employee who worked for Meghan and Harry during their time at Kensington Palace tried to describe the relationship between the couple. She paraphrased a line from George Bernard Shaw. She said, 'Just remember that in all relationships, but in this one especially, one kisses, and one allows the kiss.'

And who knows, things change over time and often have a tendency to come full circle. When the marriage of Meghan and Harry no longer excites the tabloids and the feeding frenzy has moved to some other celebrity couple, London, and specifically Kensington Palace, may not seem such a bad place to live after all. The fact that Meghan and Harry wanted to take some part of their current world with them – demonstrated by their denied wish to continue as part-time royals – speaks volumes about the difficulties of shaking off the past and embracing an entirely uncertain future. They may find fulfilment and happiness beyond the bounds of Kensington Palace and few would begrudge them that, but the history of royals in exile suggests it will not be easy.

ACKNOWLEDGEMENTS

As late as the 1950s, many grand country houses and even some large London houses were still run pretty much as they had been 200 years earlier, with teams of servants attending on a small number of highly privileged people. Maids, cooks, boot boys, butlers and gardeners worked long hours for little reward and might be sacked at a moment's notice for gossiping about the family for which they worked.

Only Kensington Palace and other royal palaces are still run along these lines, but in recent times the lawyers have been at work and non-disclosure agreements are imposed on all domestic staff to try to prevent any details of life behind the high walls entering the public domain.

I have been very lucky in that most of my interviews with domestic staff at Kensington and other palaces were conducted before these onerous contracts came into being. I would like to record my thanks to all the plucky individuals who agreed to talk to me over a period of nearly thirty years.

Without their help, the second half of this book would have been very difficult to write as it contains first-hand – and I think fascinating –

accounts of some previously unknown aspects of the intimate lives of Princess Margaret, Diana, Princess of Wales and Meghan Markle among others.

The early parts of the book by contrast rely heavily on printed and often obscure manuscript sources – for their unfailingly patient help in tracking down various items for me, I would like to thank the staff of the British Library and Kensington Central Library.

Making a book like this work really well might seem to be entirely down to the author. In fact, nothing could be further from the truth – the editor's role is absolutely vital and I would like to record my heartfelt thanks to Molly Arnold, my brilliant (and very patient) editor at Biteback, for vastly improving the final draft and for saving me from mistakes too numerous to mention.

Finally, a special thank you to my family, especially my wife Charlotte and my sons Alex, James and Joseph. My daughter Katy did a marvellous job of reading through the final version of the book and found far more errors than I am happy to admit!

BIBLIOGRAPHY

Ackroyd, Peter, *London: The Biography* (Chatto & Windus, 2000)

Ackroyd, Peter, *Revolution: A History of England Vol IV* (Macmillan, 2016)

Allen, Robert C., *Enclosure and the Yeoman* (Clarendon Press, 1992)

Appleyard, J., *William of Orange and the English Revolution* (J. M. Dent, 1908)

Bagehot, Walter, *The British Constitution*, ed. Paul Smith (Cambridge University Press, 2001)

Baldry, A. L., *Royal Palaces* (The Studio, 1935)

Beamish, Noel de Vic, *A Royal Scandal* (Robert Hale, 1966)

Berg, Maxine, *Luxury and Pleasure in Eighteenth-Century Britain* (Oxford University Press, 2005)

Bowack, John, *Antiquities of Middlesex* (W. Redmayne, 1705)

Brown, Craig, *Ma'am Darling* (Fourth Estate, 2017)

Bryant, Chris, *Entitled: A Critical History of the British Aristocracy* (Doubleday, 2007)

Castiglione, Baldassare, *The Book of the Courtier*, trans. Thomas Hoby (J. M. Dent, 1970)

Channon, Henry, *Chips: The Diaries of Sir Henry Channon* (Weidenfeld & Nicolson, 1993)

Charlton, John, *Kensington Palace: An Illustrated Guide to the State Apartments* (HMSO, 1958)

Cherry, B. and Pevsner, N., *The Buildings of England, London 3: North West* (Penguin, 1991)

Claydon, Tony and Speck, M. A., *William and Mary* (Oxford University Press, 2007)

Curzon, Catherine, *Life in the Georgian Court* (Pen & Sword, 2016)

Dempster, Nigel and Evans, Peter, *Behind Palace Doors* (Orion, 1993)

Dennison, Matthew, *Queen Victoria: A Life of Contradictions* (William Collins, 2013)

Dobson, Austin, *Old Kensington Palace and Other Papers* (Humphrey Milford, 1926)

Farson, Daniel, *The Gilded Gutter Life of Francis Bacon* (Vintage, 1994)

Faulkner, Thomas, *History and Antiquities of Kensington* (T. Egerton, 1820)

Field, Ophelia, *The Favourite: Sarah, Duchess of Marlborough* (Hodder, 2002)

Flanders, Judith, *Consuming Passions: Leisure and Pleasure in Victorian Britain* (HarperPress, 2006)

French, George Russell, *The Ancestry of Her Majesty Queen Victoria and His Royal Highness Prince Albert* (William Pickering, 1841)

Fryman, Olivia (ed.), *Kensington Palace: Art, Architecture and Society* (Yale, 2018)

Fulford, Roger, *The Wicked Uncles* (Pan, 1968)

Glasheen, Joan, *The Secret People of the Palaces* (Batsford, 1998)

Glenconner, Anne, *Lady in Waiting: My Extraordinary Life in the Shadow of the Crown* (Hodder, 2019)

Graham, Eleanor, *The Making of a Queen: Victoria at Kensington Palace* (J. Cape, 1940)

Greig, Hannah, *The Beau Monde* (Oxford University Press, 2013)

Hadlow, Janice, *The Strangest Family: The Private Lives of George III, Queen Charlotte and the Hanoverians* (William Collins, 2014)

Hamilton, Anthony, *Memoirs of the Count de Grammont* (The Bodley Head, 1928)

Hatton, Ragnhild, *George I* (Yale University Press, 1978)

Hecht, J. Jean, *The Domestic Servant Class in Eighteenth-Century England* (Routledge & Kegan Paul, 1956)

Hervey, John, *Lord Hervey's Memoirs*, ed. Romney Sedgwick (Penguin, 1984)

Hibbert, Christopher and Weinreb, Ben, *The London Encyclopaedia* (Macmillan, 1983)

Hoskins, W. G., *The Making of the English Landscape* (Penguin, 1970)

Hunt, Leigh, *The Old Court Suburb* (Hurst and Blackett, 1855)

Impey, Edward, *Kensington Palace: The Official Illustrated History* (Merrell, 2003)

Jackman, Nancy, *The Cook's Tale* (Sceptre, 2012)

Langford, Paul, *Eighteenth-Century Britain: A Very Short Introduction* (Oxford University Press, 1984)

Law, Ernest, *An Historical Guide to Kensington Palace, the Birthplace of Queen Victoria* (Hugh Rees, 1908)

Linebaugh, Peter, *Stop Thief! The Commons, Enclosures and Resistance* (PM Press, 2014)

Loftie, William John, *Kensington: Picturesque and Historical* (The Leadenhall Press, 1888)

Loftie, William John, *Kensington Palace and Gardens* (Farmer and Sons, 1900)

Malcolm, James Peller, *Anecdotes of the Manners and Customs of London during the Eighteenth Century* (Longman, Hurst, Rees & Orme, 1810)

Marot, Christopher, *Victoria's Other Self*, unpublished PhD

Melville, Lewis, *Lady Suffolk and Her Circle* (Hutchinson, 1924)

Morton, Andrew, *Inside Kensington Palace* (Michael O'Mara, 1987)

Murphy, N. T. P., *One Man's London* (Hutchinson, 1989)

Newsome, David, *The Victorian World Picture* (John Murray, 1997)

Pepys, Samuel, *The Diary of Samuel Pepys*, eds. Robert Latham and William Matthews (Bell & Hyman, 1985)

Picard, Liza, *Restoration London: Everyday Life in the 1660s* (Weidenfeld & Nicolson, 2004)

Picard, Liza, *Victorian London: The Life of a City 1840–1870* (Weidenfeld & Nicolson, 2006)

Pyne, W. H., *History of the Royal Residences* (A. Dry, 1819)

Quinn, Tom, *The Maid's Tale* (Coronet, 2011)

Quinn, Tom, *The Butler's Tale* (Coronet, 2012)

Quinn, Tom, *Backstairs Billy: The Life of William Tallon* (Biteback Publishing, 2015)

Quinn, Tom, *Mrs Keppel: Mistress to the King* (Biteback Publishing, 2016)

Rait, R. S., *Royal Palaces of England* (1911)

Ridley, Jane, *Bertie: A life of Edward VII* (Chatto & Windus, 2012)

Robertson-Scott, J. W., *The Story of the Pall Mall Gazette* (Oxford University Press, 1950)

Russell, Bertrand, *The Autobiography of Bertrand Russell: 1872–1914* (Allen & Unwin, 1967)

de Saussure, César-François, *A Foreign View of England in 1725–1729*, trans. M. van Muyden (John Murray, 1902)

Shaw, Karl, *Eccentrics and Oddballs* (Robinson, 2000)

Simms, R. S., *Kensington Palace* (HMSO, 1936)

Somerset, Anne, *Queen Anne: The Politics of Passion* (HarperPress, 2012)

Stockmar, Baron Christian Friedrich, *Memoirs of Baron Stockmar*, ed. Baron E. Stockmar, trans. F. M. Muller (Longmans, Green & Co., 1872)

Strachey, Lytton, *Eminent Victorians* (Chatto & Windus, 1918)

Strachey, Lytton, *Queen Victoria* (Chatto & Windus, 1921)

Thackeray, William Makepeace, *The Four Georges and the English Humourists* (Alan Sutton, 1995)

Thomas, Keith, *The Ends of Life: Roads to Fulfilment in Early Modern England* (Oxford University Press, 2009)

Thomson, Katherine, *Memoirs of Viscountess Sundon* (Henry Colburn, 1847)

Thorold, Peter, *The London Rich: The Creation of a Great City, from 1666 to the Present* (Viking, 1999)

Tinniswood, Adrian, *His Invention So Fertile: A Life of Sir Christopher Wren* (Jonathan Cape, 2001)

Tinniswood, Adrian, *Behind the Throne: A Domestic History of the Royal Household* (Vintage, 2018)

Trevelyan, George Macaulay, *The England of Queen Anne* (Longmans, Green & Co., 1932)

Troost, Wout, *William III, The Stadholder-King: A Political Biography* (Routledge, 2005)

Van der Kiste, John, *William and Mary: Heroes of the Glorious Revolution* (The History Press, 2008)

Vansittart, Peter, *London: A Literary Companion* (John Murray, 1992)

Vickery, Amanda, *The Gentleman's Daughter: Women's Lives in Georgian England* (Yale University Press, 1998)

Vickery, Amanda, *Behind Closed Doors: At Home in Georgian England* (Yale University Press, 2009)

Queen Victoria, *Leaves from the Journal of Our Life in the Highlands, from 1841 to 1868* (Smith, Elder & Company, 1868)

Queen Victoria, *The Letters of Queen Victoria*, eds. Arthur Christopher Benson and Viscount Esher (John Murray, 1908)

Walford, Edward, *Old and New London* (Cassell, Petter and Galpin, 1878)

Walpole, Horace, *Reminiscences* (Oxford University Press, 1924)

Weintraub, Stanley, *Victoria: Biography of a Queen* (HarperCollins, 1987)

Weintraub, Stanley, *Albert: Uncrowned King* (John Murray, 1997)

Wells, John, *The House of Lords* (Hodder, 1997)

Whitaker-Wilson, Cecil, *Sir Christopher Wren: His Life and Times* (Methuen & Company, 1932)

Williams-Wynn, Frances, *Diaries of a Lady of Quality: From 1794 to 1844* (Longman, Green, Longman, Roberts & Green, 1864)

Wilson, A. N., *Victoria: A Life* (Atlantic Books, 2014)

Worsley, Lucy, *Courtiers: The Secret History of Kensington Palace* (Faber & Faber, 2010)

ABOUT THE AUTHOR

© Katy Guest

Tom Quinn is the author of *The Reluctant Billionaire: The Tragic Life of Gerald Grosvenor, Sixth Duke of Westminster*; *Mrs Keppel: Mistress to the King*; *Backstairs Billy: The Life of William Tallon, the Queen Mother's Most Devoted Servant*; *Cocoa at Midnight: The True Story of My Life as a Housekeeper*; *The Cook's Tale: Life Below Stairs as It Really Was* and many more titles.

He lives in London.

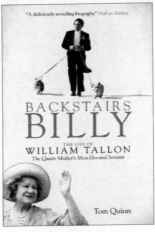

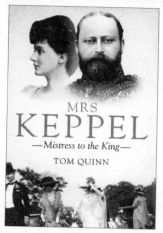